Unlocking the Potential of Team-Based Staffing

Unlocking the Potential of Team-Based Staffing

A Guide for School and System Leaders

BRENT W. MADDIN
R. LENNON AUDRAIN
LISA MARESSO WYATT
KAYCEE SALMACIA

HARVARD EDUCATION PRESS
CAMBRIDGE, MASSACHUSETTS

Paperback ISBN 9798895570067

Library of Congress Cataloging-in-Publication Data is on file.

Published by Harvard Education Press,
an imprint of the Harvard Education Publishing Group

Harvard Education Press
8 Story Street
Cambridge, MA 02138

Cover Design: Jackie Shepherd Design
Cover Image: New Africa via Shutterstock

The typefaces in this book are Adobe Garamond Pro and Myriad Pro.

We'd like to dedicate this book to the educational leaders who, together with their communities, bravely built team-based staffing models before there were resources to reference and models to observe.

Contents

Contents

Foreword

In my earlier career as a high-school teacher, I learned firsthand that the way that a school is set up, designed, and managed is crucial. Poorly designed and run schools made it difficult and stressful, if not impossible, for us teachers to do the job successfully. On the other hand, well-run schools fostered and enabled our work and made the job of teaching deeply satisfying. Later, when I began my career as a researcher and professor, I learned that my experiences and insights were not unique. I found, not surprisingly, that how to design and set up the good school—a school that works well for both students and teachers—has long been a subject of great interest to education scholars, reformers, and practitioners. In short, it has long been recognized that the design and organization of schools matter.

One of the most contentious aspects of the design of schooling has been the conventional classroom model—one-teacher, one-classroom, with twenty-five to thirty-five students. In his classic work on teachers, Dan Lortie described this as an "egg crate" model, in which large numbers of the once-predominant one-room schoolhouses were consolidated under one roof. Historians have documented how this model was widely implemented over a century ago with the creation of the public school system. Funded by taxpayers, the public education system had the goal of delivering universal, uniform education services to a mass base of "customers" at the lowest possible cost. Borrowing from industrial production models, such as Henry Ford's famous assembly line, schools were designed as rows of separate identical classroom units through which students are conveyed in age-graded batches. That has been the norm since.

Despite its ubiquity, many educational researchers, practitioners, and reformers have long argued that the conventional classroom design is ill fitted to the education of the young and ill fitted to the work of teaching. Going back to John Dewey, educational theory has long held that students' learning is optimized when teachers are able to tailor their instruction to individual students' needs; this is often called "student-centered" or "personalized" education. Instruction imparting deeper engagement and learning to students has been akin to something of a "holy grail"—a noble goal to which teachers are to aspire. For several reasons, however, this aspiration typically collides with reality.

One reason for this is that teachers must simultaneously work with relatively large numbers of students. In many human-services and caring occupations and professions, practitioners work with individual clients or small groups of clients at a time. In contrast, in the typical school system, teachers work with large groups of student-clients. For departmentalized settings such as secondary schools, this might mean that a teacher serves 125–150 individuals per day on average.

Not only do educational systems require teachers to work simultaneously with large numbers of individuals, but the students come to school with a wide variety of backgrounds, needs, abilities, and levels of motivation and preparation. Yet schools and teachers are obligated to educate *all* youngsters, regardless of how prepared, motivated, or cooperative they are.

Along with serving multiple and varied students, the teaching job in school systems requires educators to achieve multiple goals for these students. There has long been little consensus, and much disagreement, across society regarding what the goals and end products of schooling ought to be. This is not surprising, given that schools are institutions created to serve the public and their children and are funded and governed through local school boards and state legislatures. The public not only is legally entitled to a voice in local schooling, but also has widely varying, and sometimes competing, views of what the role of their schools ought to be. Hence, the public has multiple, and sometimes competing, ideas for what teachers are expected to do with their children. Typical lists of these expectations are long, including building basic literacy skills (reading, math, writing, speaking); encouraging academic excellence; developing occupational or vocational skills; promoting good work habits and self-discipline; ensuring personal socioemotional growth; developing human relations skills; inculcating specific moral values; enhancing social justice and multicultural awareness, and still other goals. Addressing these many goals is a daunting task for any teacher.

Finally, there is another aspect of the work of teaching in school systems that makes the conventional classroom a difficult environment for teaching and learning. The multiyear process of educating the young in school systems is inherently interdependent, collaborative, and collective work, requiring groups of teachers to work together as teams. However, the conventional classroom means that the work of teaching is done largely in isolation from colleagues.

In short, the conventional classroom design requires teachers to achieve multiple goals, with large numbers of individual students who have a wide variety of backgrounds, needs, abilities, and levels of motivation and preparation, and to do all this isolated and alone in one's own classroom. Not surprisingly, teachers often find it very difficult to meet their students' needs in the conventional classroom setting, and not surprisingly, this conventional model of schooling has long been the target of reform.

The focus of this book is a new alternative to the conventional model, entitled the Next Education Workforce initiative. It entails an innovative redesign of the way that classrooms are set up and staffed. Rather than individual, isolated teachers, each with a large number of students in a single classroom, the Next Education Workforce model deploys integrated teams of teaching staff, who share a roster of students, share multiple learning spaces, and collectively plan their teaching, with each member having a different role and responsibilities. Next Education Workforce teams adjust their schedule according to the needs of students, group their students based on their needs and interests, use data to tailor learning to each student, and provide each student with rigorous learning opportunities. In short, this model seeks to make deeper, personalized student-centered teaching and learning possible and sustainable and, ultimately, to improve the motivation and learning of students and the performance, job satisfaction, and retention of teachers.

To accomplish this, the Next Education Workforce model brings together in a unique, integrated package several long-standing school design components and reform ideas: partnerships between higher-education and schools, team teaching, distributed-expertise staffing, beginning teacher induction/support, faculty professional development, and enhanced teacher discretion and "voice" with regard to instructional decisions.

This new team-based staffing model deserves attention, and indeed in the past several years, it has spread to over 150 schools in fifty school districts. As a welcome aid to this growing movement, this book provides a much-needed summary of the vision and theory behind the model, the growing body of evidence supporting it, and guidance on how to go about setting it up. Thinking back to my earlier life as a high-school teacher, the Next Education Workforce is just the kind of thoughtful experiment that I would have loved to have been a part of and now would love to see further develop, spread, and succeed.

Richard M. Ingersoll
Professor of Education and Sociology
University of Pennsylvania

Introduction

In most schools today, a problematic tension exists. Schools must be places that provide experiences that students find worth doing while also ensuring that delivering those experiences is doable for teachers.[1]

Student-centered approaches to teaching and learning help school be *worth doing* for learners. Yet we also know that meeting the academic and socioemotional needs of every learner is an incredibly challenging task for one educator to achieve with the twenty-five to 150 students they serve. Yet we expect the 3.5 million teachers in the United States to rise to this challenge every day. Is this really *doable*?

Given the intense challenges of being an educator in today's classrooms, it shouldn't be surprising to learn that for more than a decade, fewer people were enrolling in teacher preparation programs, teachers are currently exiting the profession at alarming rates, and the teacher workforce is younger and less experienced than at any point in recent history.[2]

In spring 2022, as we entered the third year of the COVID-19 pandemic, the teacher workforce was in an even more precarious state. Only 56 percent of US teachers reported that they were satisfied with their jobs.[3] In a 2022 survey, the National Education Association found that 55 percent of their members reported they were considering leaving the teaching profession at the end of the 2021–2022 school year, and around 8 percent of educators actually did leave the profession, matching historical trends.[4] These statistics are even more dire in schools serving students who come from low-income backgrounds and identify as students of color who face greater disparities in access to experienced educators, rigorous coursework, and academic support.[5] The data are clear: educators are not thriving, and the overall health of the education profession is poor.

WORKFORCE DESIGN

When other fields face similar workforce challenges, they engage in *workforce design*, which focuses on effectively managing human capital.[6] The overarching goal of workforce design is "to have the right people with the right skills in the right job at the right time performing their assignments efficiently and effectively."[7] In health care, workforce design created opportunities for new roles and responsibilities for the field's workers.[8] The health-care industry also changed the way that people worked with one another, moving away from traditional ways of delivering health care toward multidisciplinary teams.[9]

Workforce design forced health care to examine the structures and rules that organized the field's work and built a new design to meet the needs of its workforce and clients. In education, while many have attempted to challenge the "structures and rules that organized the work" of schooling to better meet the needs of educators and learners, these efforts have been relatively unsuccessful.[10] This lack of success is not for lack of trying; rather, those structures and rules—also commonly known as the *grammar of schooling*—make changing the status quo very difficult.[11]

THE GRAMMAR OF SCHOOLING

The *grammar of schooling* is defined as the "structures and rules that organize the work" of schooling.[12] One of the most central rules within this framework is the normative way that we staff schools: one teacher per classroom. In most American schools, the grammar of schooling manifests as a model where twenty-five or more students, grouped by age or ability, are being instructed by one teacher, in a single classroom, who is alone and isolated for most of the day.[13] Students stay with that single individual either all day, in elementary settings, or until a bell rings, in secondary schools; and we ask that single teacher to be all things to all learners at all times. A teacher's job is incredibly hard even before committing to deliver deeper and personalized learning to all students.

The grammar of schooling has also been characterized as the "organizational framework that shapes the conditions under which teachers instruct students."[14] Emerick and his colleagues succinctly summarize these conditions as follows:

"Teachers often are isolated in their classrooms, face overwhelming noninstructional duties, have extremely limited opportunities for meaningful decision making, lack basic instructional materials, and perceive few opportunities for advancement and growth."[15]

Some believe that the grammar of schooling itself needs to change before any other improvements to schooling can take place.[16] We agree, and we contend that rethinking the way that we staff schools is a crucial first step in addressing both the structural and organizational dimensions of the typical grammar of schooling. To change the learning experiences that students have, we must first address—and revise—the traditional staffing structures embedded in the grammar of schooling.

THE CASE FOR RETHINKING SCHOOL STAFFING

The COVID-19 pandemic provided many reasons to redesign the traditional grammar of schooling, and specifically the one-teacher, one-classroom model of staffing. First, there is mounting evidence that many students, and especially our most vulnerable learners, were not served well during the pandemic. However, the quality of educational experiences already had been falling short before the pandemic. Shutdowns and fragmented learning only exacerbated these trends. These data, combined with the relatively flat and almost universally underwhelming measures of academic achievement both prepandemic and postpandemic, suggest that many students have not had access to types of educational experiences that will prepare them for success in college, career, community, and life. While the COVID-19 pandemic wasn't the first cry for redesign (such calls had been coming for decades), it served as a focusing event, attracting the attention of diverse groups concerned about educational outcomes.

The second reason to redesign school staffing models is educators' growing dissatisfaction with their jobs and waning commitment to the profession. Even prior to the pandemic, colleges of education were seeing declining enrollments of more than one-third over the previous decade, and respect for the profession was at an all-time low.[17]

Notably, these two reasons are linked. Labaree argues that schooling must balance being worth doing and doable.[18] "Worth doing" speaks to the learning opportunities and pedagogical approaches experienced by learners, while "doable" speaks to the organizational approaches of teachers and learners in schools. For example, if schools focus only on implementing new instructional and pedagogical approaches to improve student engagement and outcomes while ignoring the organizational impediments to implementation, school may be worth doing but not doable.

Conversely, if schools focus on changing how the individuals who work in schools are organized without changing their instructional and pedagogical approaches to meet the needs of learners, schooling may be doable but not worth doing. Ultimately, to deliver equitable learning outcomes for learners and to make teachers' jobs more satisfying and sustainable, fundamental aspects of the grammar of schooling must change.

MAKING SCHOOLING WORTH DOING

Deeper Learning

Policy makers, families, and members of the community are calling for schools to deliver deeper learning experiences to prepare students for "the demands of life, work, and citizenship . . . which will enable students to think critically, solve problems, use knowledge for new purposes, and learn how to learn."[19] To embrace the multiplicative identities of an increasingly diverse student population, many communities across the country have called for curricular and pedagogical approaches that are more culturally sustaining.[20]

Despite the demand, deeper learning experiences are the exception, not the rule, in most American schools. *Deeper learning* is a form of student-centered learning grounded in theorists like Lev Vygotsky and John Dewey.[21] There are six deeper learning competencies to assist learners in developing deep understandings of academic content: "(1) mastery of core academic content; (2) critical thinking and problem solving; (3) effective communication; (4) ability to work collaboratively; (5) learning how to learn; [and] (6) academic mindsets."[22] Deeper learning is a pedagogical approach that meets the various social demands of education. The purpose is to "equip students with the skills to find, analyze, and apply knowledge in new and emerging contexts and situations," and to prepare students for "college, work, civic participation in a democratic society, and lifelong learning in a fast-changing and information-rich world."[23] In practical terms, this might look like students engaging in project-based learning in school, where they investigate real-world issues, work in teams to develop solutions, and present their findings to peers, teachers, and community members. For instance, a science class might not only learn about environmental sustainability but also partner with local organizations to design and implement small-scale projects, such as creating a school garden or participating in waste-reduction initiatives.

Personalized Learning

The term *personalized learning* often conjures imagery of educational technology that adapts to students' learning needs. However, as defined by the US Department of Education, personalized learning is not about the means of the delivery, but rather the pedagogical orientation that instruction should reflect learners' needs and be tailored to students' learning preferences and specific interests.[24] In an environment that is fully personalized, the learning objectives, content, method, and pace may all vary.

Personalized learning is complex, and researchers and practitioners alike conceptualize and implement personalized learning in various ways.[25] Personalized learning does not have a specific set of practices that a school can adopt; instead, human, institutional, and instructional resources typically drive how such learning is implemented.[26] Evidence suggests that experiences using personalized learning approaches, in its many implementations, are associated with positive academic outcomes and attitudes toward learning.[27]

Centering Relationships

The pursuit of deeper and personalized learning alone is likely not enough to make school worth doing for students. Central to the art of teaching—and supported by a growing scientific research base—are relationships, which form a vital cornerstone of learning.[28] In fact, it is the quality of the relationships between students and their educators that cement the worthiness of this pursuit. When students feel seen, understood, and supported by educators who invest in them personally and academically, their motivation and capacity to learn expand significantly.

These relationships foster an environment where students are more willing to take risks, ask questions, and engage deeply with content, creating a sense of belonging that makes school truly meaningful. Any work that we undertake to address the grammar of schooling must strive to make school inherently worth doing. However, this work must place relationships at the center, ensuring that, while redesigning structures, we do not lose the human connections that drive engagement, resilience, and love of learning.

Making Schooling Worth Doing by Making It Doable

Organizational demands. We know that schools need to deliver learning experiences to students that are worth doing, but as the grammar of schooling is currently designed, it is not doable for educators. If schools are to meet the demand for deeper and personalized learning—while not compromising relationships—they must change how they are organized to deliver these experiences.

Teaching is a complex task.[29] A single teacher, in isolation, is responsible for planning for instruction, moving their group of twenty-five (or more) students through the required curriculum, assessing students, and reflecting on practices.[30] Over the decades, all these tasks have caused policy makers and researchers to question the doability of teaching. Many other industries, such as health care, have transitioned from individual experts responsible for executing one complex task to decomposing that task and redistributing it to multiple members in teams.[31] As schools work toward transforming their grammar of schooling by incorporating more complex pedagogical approaches, such as deeper learning and personalized learning, they should also consider creating team-based staffing models, as other industries have done when facing similar complex tasks.

Changing the grammar of schooling is not easy, especially for schools stuck in the existing paradigm. Since 2018, we have been working with educational leaders and their communities to design, launch, and sustain new staffing models that enable the job to be more doable for educators so they can deliver experiences to students that they find worth doing.

THE NEXT EDUCATION WORKFORCE INITIATIVE

Beginning in 2018, the Next Education Workforce initiative at Arizona State University (ASU)'s Mary Lou Fulton College for Teaching and Learning Innovation has been working in partnership with schools and school systems to fundamentally redesign how we staff schools. Our work starts with the belief that for school to be worth doing, all students should have access to—and enjoy equitable outcomes from—deeper and more personalized learning experiences. To make that work doable, teachers should be staffed as teams of educators with distributed expertise who share the same roster of students. To emphasize the concrete mechanism for transformation, we describe our work as building Next Education Workforce team-based staffing models.

The Growing Evidence Base for Next Education Workforce Models

As of fall 2024, more than 140 schools from nearly fifty school systems across seventeen states are implementing Next Education Workforce team-based staffing models. In addition to beginning to achieve national scale, these models are associated with promising outcomes for learners and educators alike. In a study conducted by Johns Hopkins University's Institute for Education Policy, researchers found that teachers in Next Education Workforce models are statistically significantly ($p < 0.05$) more satisfied, collaborate more, and have better teacher-student interactions than educators in traditional classroom models.[32] Researchers from Johns Hopkins University also found that Next Education Workforce teachers were more engaged, requesting fewer substitutes and days off, than their counterparts in traditional staffing structures.[33] Findings from a study conducted by the Center on Reinventing Public Education indicate that teachers in Next Education Workforce models have higher retention rates, longer career plans, increased satisfaction, and improved evaluations.[34] Research also indicates that teachers in Next Education Workforce models report higher levels of autonomy and lower turnover rates compared to the traditionally staffed counterparts.[35] Finally, evidence suggests that teachers in Next Education Workforce models are more likely to report better professional working conditions (i.e., professional learning, professional trust, contributions to school-level decision making, and respect) and self-efficacy.[36]

Statistically significant differences were also found in student outcomes. When examining reading growth for more than 3,000 third-grade students, researchers found these learners make 1.4 years of reading growth in a single year in Next Education Workforce models, compared to 1.01 years of reading growth for students in traditional classroom models on average.[37] Finally, researchers found that ninth-grade students in Next Education Workforce models passed Algebra 1 at a 4-percentage-point higher rate than comparable peers in the same district on average.[38] In the same sample, female students served by teams passed Algebra 1 at a 7-percentage-point higher rate than female students in traditional staffing models.[39]

The evidence base will continue to grow, but these are promising signs that Next Education Workforce team-based staffing models are associated with positive outcomes for both educators and students.

The Next Education Workforce as an Example of Strategic School Staffing

In 2023, a group of funders commissioned Education First to conduct a landscape scan to map innovative work related to the education workforce.[40] One outcome of the scan was a new term, *strategic school staffing*, which includes work that "reimagines the teaching profession by disrupting the one-teacher, one-classroom model and replaces it with innovative solutions . . . to improve student learning outcomes and make the teaching profession more sustainable."[41]

Based on interviews with organizations supporting the redesign of the education workforce, Education First identified six characteristics of strategic school staffing: "(1) distributed leadership; (2) compensation structures differentiated by role; (3) innovative teaming structures; (4) extended teacher reach; (5) staffing structures that intentionally cultivate teacher pipelines; and (6) technology that optimizes educator roles and time."[42] While Next Education Workforce models commonly include all these characteristics to a greater or lesser degree, the defining characteristic of our models is the innovative teaming structure, in which teachers are "collectively accountable for student success, with intentional consideration of the differentiated roles within teams that are needed to support this structure."[43]

Within their landscape scan, Education First identified the Next Education Workforce initiative and a handful of other organizations that support schools and school systems to change how teaching teams are structured to better support students.[44] Of those organizations, it is worth noting that Public Impact, a national technical assistance provider, and its Opportunity Culture model is the only other strategic school staffing model that has achieved notable scale with a model related to rethinking educator roles. As of 2024, more than 800 schools across thirteen states since 2013 have used Opportunity Culture models.[45] Despite important differences between our models, we are united in the belief that the way that we staff schools must change and our organizations collaborate frequently to that end.[46]

But Isn't This Just Team Teaching from the 1960s?

Many readers will rightly ask if strategic school staffing is related to team teaching from the 1960s.[47] In fact, as historians of education note, from the 1950s through the 1970s, American education focused on reforming the instructional and organizational features of schooling.

Between the end of World War II and the onset of the Cold War in 1947, there was growing concern over the academic preparedness of American students. The Soviet Union's launching of Sputnik in 1957 increased the interest of families, policy makers, and school leaders in redesigning the schooling experience to prepare American students to be globally competitive. As a result of the baby boom, schools were growing larger and more complex, and new technologies, such as televisions and audiovisual aids, offered new horizons for delivering instruction and individualizing student learning. Through team teaching, educators would be able to better capitalize on these advancements. One of the earliest team teaching models was the Lexington Team Teaching Project in Massachusetts, which began in 1957. Supported by the Harvard Graduate School of Education and the Ford Foundation, Lexington's team teaching model included multiple educators who utilized flexible classroom spaces and structured their school in multiple age groups.

Educational reformers in the twentieth century called for a redesign of physical classroom space, multiple educators being responsible for larger groups of students, and an end to the traditional age-graded classroom. Taken together, these changes to the grammar of schooling were called "team teaching."

Learning from History

It is not lost on us that we are now reviving a movement that started at Harvard's education school and publishing a book through its press. We believe that there is a renewed urgency around the work to redesign schools that deliver learning worth doing and to enable the job to be more doable for educators.

While our team-based staffing models have similarities and differences compared to the team teaching models of the 1950s–1970s, we take our history lessons seriously so we avoid repeating the mistakes of the past. While there were significant challenges that ultimately led to team teaching's decline, we also believe that conditions today are markedly different. Advances in technology have increased our ability to communicate, share data, collaboratively plan, and adapt learning in real time. Technology like this did not exist in the 1960s.

Policy is also now incentivizing professional learning through a collaborative lens. For instance, Title II of the Every Student Succeeds Act of 2015 (the reauthorization of the Elementary and Secondary Education Act) now encourages professional development that is "sustained (not stand-alone, one-day, or short term workshops), intensive, collaborative, job-embedded, data-driven, and classroom-focused."[48] Policy language like this did not exist in the mid-twentieth century.

In the late 1960s and early 1970s, however, team teaching became a target of criticism not because of its own merits or drawbacks, but due to its tight coupling with broader progressive-era reforms. Reformers seeking to push back against what they saw as the excesses of progressive education used team teaching as a scapegoat.

However, team teaching itself was not merely a progressive reform effort, but a fundamental shift in how schools could be organized to better support what we now know about learners and learning. Far from being a relic of progressive reform, team teaching aligns with contemporary research about how to best support students, such as multitiered systems of support (MTSS), science of learning and development, and socioemotional learning. Team teaching also fundamentally strengthens Richard Elmore's concept of the instructional core by maximizing the interdependent relationships among teachers, students, and content.[49]

Finally, one of the last reasons why team teaching declined was that it lacked a clear definition.[50] There were too many varieties of team teaching floating around in the mid-twentieth century, requiring those interested in building team teaching models to spend "endless hours analyzing the variety of team teaching ideas."[51] With all of this in mind, we feel a particular urgency in more formally codifying, in the form of this book, what we have learned in supporting educational leaders as they design, launch, and scale Next Education Workforce team-based staffing models.

OVERVIEW OF THE BOOK

Having worked in partnership with educators from school systems across the country to build Next Education Workforce models, we have come to see patterns associated with the successful design and launch of team-based staffing models. This book captures those learnings and distills them into concrete actions for school leaders looking to improve student and educator outcomes. Educational policy makers, governing board members, teacher leaders, and advocates for education will also benefit from reading this book to understand the need for—and how to design—team-based staffing models.

A Note on Resources on Our Authors' Page

Throughout this book, we mention resources available on our Harvard Education Press Authors' Page, though these are not an exhaustive list of the resources that are available. We encourage you to visit and explore this page while you read this book. We anticipate adding more resources aligned to each chapter after the printing of this book.

A Note on Nomenclature

While we often use consistent words and phrases throughout this book, there are cases in which we, or our school partners, use different language. Table 0.1 lists our preferred terminology and synonyms.

TABLE 0.1 Terms used in this book and synonyms that the reader may encounter

What we mostly use	*But you might also see*
Team-based staffing models	Team-based models, strategic school staffing models, Next Education Workforce models, Next Education Workforce team-based models
First team	First model, pilot model, pilot team, initial team
Lead Teachers	Team leads, teacher leader, Teacher Executive Designer, Transformational Teacher Leader

A Note on the Location of the Schools Mentioned in This Book

Unless otherwise noted, the schools referenced in this book are located in Arizona. This is where the work of Next Education Workforce team-based staffing has been underway the longest, and the individuals from these schools and systems provide a rich foundation for insights and lessons learned. The educators and leaders featured here offer reflections on their experiences—what they wish they had known when they first began—so that others embarking on a similar journey can benefit from their hindsight and expertise.

Why We Talk About Building Your "First Team" in the Singular

Throughout the book, we reference building your "first team." On one hand, this is a stylistic choice to make the book more readable. But on the other hand, this also has a distinct purpose. Having supported hundreds of school leaders in their design and launch of team-based staffing models, we have witnessed firsthand the power of starting small, with a single team or two. When that first team experiences success, we have seen interest in, and demand for, team-based staffing growth within communities.

A single, cohesive team enables school leaders to concentrate their efforts, resources, and energy on supporting this team and creating a more manageable implementation process. This enables school leaders to refine ideas, address challenges, and identify and remove potential barriers before teams scale across their sites. A first team helps educators and school leaders build confidence in team-based staffing and generate small wins and evidence of success, and it also can set the stage for scaled implementation.

Overview of the Chapters

The purpose of this book is to provide school leaders—broadly defined as anyone who has substantial decision-making power or influence at a school site—with a guide to preparing to launch Next Education Workforce team-based staffing models. The book is divided into eight chapters, with chapters 1–7 focused on launching your first team and chapter 8 serving as a short guide to the considerations that you might make as you plan to scale team-based staffing at your school.

Chapter 1: From teacher-of-record to team-of-record. Teacher-of-record is the term used to describe the relationship between a teacher and the roster of students. It is the operationalization of the one-teacher, one-classroom model. This chapter describes what we mean when we say that we are moving away from a teacher-of-record and toward a team-of-record, where educators work collaboratively to support a shared roster of students. Chapter 1 will provide you with sample team-based models that vary in complexity. In this chapter, we also explore key shifts that occur when transitioning to team-based models: shifts in working conditions, teaching and learning, relationships, and the ways that teachers enter, specialize, and advance in the profession.

Chapter 2: Identifying **why** ***a team-based model makes sense in your context.*** Crystalizing your *why for teaming* is a crucial first step as you begin to design team-based staffing models. This chapter presents the stories of three school leaders and how they determined why a team-based model made sense in their respective contexts. We also discuss how Boyd's Ecology Framework is a useful tool for thinking about the components that might drive your *why for teaming.*

Chapter 3: Change management for your first team. Launching team-based staffing models requires carefully executed change management. This chapter provides multiple frames for thinking about the change management process, including Kotter's Change Model, Diffusion of Innovation, and Technical and Adaptive Change. This chapter highlights stories of how school leaders navigated and led change management as they were building their first teams.

Chapter 4: Building your first team. The success of your first team hinges on its thoughtful design. This chapter offers practical strategies and suggestions for initial educator team design. School leaders should consider their *why for teaming*, determine who the shared roster of students will be, figure out the expertise needed to meet learners' strengths and needs, and decide how to select educators to join your first team who have the collective expertise to meet those needs. This chapter also addresses the benefits and challenges associated with launching more than one team and how to best support teams once they launch.

Chapter 5: Building the master schedule to support team-based staffing. In this chapter, we discuss the critical role of the master schedule for implementing your first team. A well-designed master schedule is a mechanism that enables collaborative planning time and common instructional time. This chapter offers strategies for school leaders as they redesign their master schedules and includes sample master schedules for elementary and secondary schools. It also explains how to build a master schedule to maximize the effectiveness of teams and introduce more flexibility to incorporate community educators and create instructional plans for diverse students. We describe the conversations, constraints, unintended consequences, and trade-offs that school leaders must make as they build a master schedule to meet the needs of educator teams.

Chapter 6: Creating shared, flexible learning environments. This chapter focuses on rethinking the physical spaces within schools to better support an educator team. Traditional classroom assignments and setups are often challenges for educator teams, but small changes can enable teams to collaborate better. Prioritizing educator proximity, designing for flexibility, and supporting shifts in the use of new space are three considerations that school leaders use as they launch their first team-based model.

Chapter 7: Team-based staffing in a world of one-teacher, one-classroom systems and structures. This chapter examines the various systems and structures that reinforce the one-teacher, one-classroom model. We explore systems associated with students and families, educators, and school operations. We also provide tangible strategies to address common infrastructural challenges associated with topics, including but not limited to family communication, family-teacher conferences, team appreciation, professional learning, educator coaching, taking attendance, and managing student data.

Chapter 8: Scaling team-based staffing. This chapter is designed to guide school leaders who have successfully launched their initial team-based staffing model and are considering how to scale teams in year two and beyond. The chapter is structured as a reexamination of the concepts introduced in chapters 2–7 and provides insights and lessons learned from other schools that have moved from one team to multiple teams.

CONCLUSION

Now more than ever, our schools face unprecedented challenges: systemic failures more exposed by the COVID-19 pandemic, a teaching profession plagued by troubles with recruitment and retention, and students whose outcomes and well-being are on the line. We believe that team-based staffing models offer a powerful response to these issues that makes schooling both *doable* for teachers and *worth doing* for students. Our commitment to this approach is resolute because the data—and our experiences with schools nationwide that have launched models in their local context—show promise for impact. By investing in teams, we're not just envisioning a better future for education—we're building it, one team at a time. We hope that this book will provide you with inspiration and resources to design and launch your first team.

CHAPTER 1

From Teacher-of-Record to Team-of-Record

In the classic grammar of schooling, teacher-of-record is the term used to describe the relationship between educators and their responsibility for instructing specific rosters of students at a given time. For elementary grades, the teacher-of-record is often the teacher with whom students spend the majority of their day. This teacher is typically responsible for planning and delivering instruction for all core content areas (e.g., math, English, science, and social studies), but not usually for electives such as physical education, art, and music.

In secondary school contexts, the teacher-of-record usually plans and delivers instruction in a content area such as science and may teach specific courses such as biology and chemistry. Students rotate between multiple teachers throughout the day. In both elementary and secondary cases, an educator is expected to be expert in specific content areas, along with myriad other responsibilities, including communicating with families, integrating new technologies, using data to drive instruction, and completing paperwork associated with students' individualized education programs—just to name a few.

Whether working in an elementary or secondary school context, teachers-of-record often feel that they must be all things to all learners at all times. Teachers feel isolated, have limited opportunities for collaboration, and are solely responsible for the outcomes of their roster of students. For a job that is so people-centered, being a teacher is a remarkably lonely profession marked by increasingly deep feelings of dissatisfaction and burnout.[1]

But it doesn't have to be this way. A paradigm shift in the way that we staff schools—from *teachers-of-record* to *teams-of-record*—is beginning to take hold in communities across the United States and around the world.

WHAT TEAMS ARE—AND WHAT THEY AREN'T

Some may argue that teachers work in team-based organizational structures right now. Educators may identify as belonging to grade-level teams, department teams, and professional learning communities (PLCs). Yet, according to the organizational and industrial psychology literature, these organizational structures embody the characteristics of work groups, not teams. While all teams are work groups—a collection of individuals who work together in some capacity—all work groups are not teams.[2]

Teams are distinguished by specific attributes. For a work group to be considered a team, it must have seven characteristics. Teams must be composed of:

- two or more individuals who
- socially interact,
- possess one or more common goals,
- are brought together to perform organizationally relevant tasks,
- exhibit interdependencies with respect to workflow, goals, and outcomes,
- have different roles and responsibilities, and
- are embedded together in an encompassing organizational system, with boundaries and links to the broader system context and task environment.[3]

Grade-level teams, department teams, and PLCs, among others, are work groups, but they do not meet all these characteristics and requirements of teams.

Many schools' work groups are indeed composed of two or more individuals who socially interact. The actual act of instruction, however, is typically conducted by a single, isolated educator in relation to a sole roster of students.[4] In addition, while these collaborative structures may share a common goal—such as increased achievement by all students—and, through the organizational structure, bring educators together to perform organizationally relevant tasks (e.g., lesson planning and writing common assessments), the team members are not interdependent. That is, the responsibility for meeting the common goal of increased student achievement is orchestrated by teachers independently, and teachers are typically measured against their influence on their roster of students' achievement.

Finally, while it is true that educators are embedded in an encompassing organizational system—their school—they rarely have different roles and responsibilities from each other. A first-year fourth-grade teacher has, on average, the same role and responsibilities as a teacher with ten years of experience—planning, instructing, assessing, reflecting, and repeating the process for a roster of students. In this way, the current organizational structure of the school assumes independent, equal effectiveness from educator to educator.[5] While many educators might characterize their collaborative structures as teams, it is evident that they do not meet all the requirements to be a team.

Another Way to Think About Teams

Randy Mahlerwein, assistant superintendent of secondary schools in Mesa Public Schools, provides another way to think about how teachers primarily collaborate in work groups and not in teams. "Imagine for a moment that teachers are like a football team," he says. "These teachers may practice together for an hour or so each day (if they're lucky), but they go play the game on their own. That's how we've organized our teachers in education today. They meet in PLCs, or at lunch, or before or after school, and then they go and play the game by themselves. With educator teams, we are talking about practicing together *and* playing the actual game together."

Schools have moved some aspects of instructional practice into collaborative structures. For example, some educators plan together with their PLCs. The scope and complexity of what is expected of each individual educator, however, are not considerably reduced even when working together. To reduce the complexity, schools must redistribute the components of the job among members of a team, known as *task shifting*.[6] Task shifting has been utilized by healthcare teams for the past decade and involves the redistribution of responsibilities among team members to optimize the use of available human resources.[7] Task shifting enables tasks to be reassigned in ways that enhance efficiency and ensure that each team member contributes according to their expertise.

While this sort of task shifting can be helpful in educational settings for relatively simple tasks (e.g., shifting lunch duties and photocopying), it can also look like sharing complex aspects of the job with other professional educators (e.g., sending one family letter home from the team instead of each teacher sending one). Deconstructing the work of teaching and redistributing the subtasks through task shifting would then make the tasks interconnected. This task interconnectedness would create team member interdependence and move a school's current work groups toward becoming teams.

Even in the current grammar of schooling, there is promising evidence to suggest that moving toward teams of educators who collaborate and share a roster of students is beneficial. For instance, when a specific set of teachers shares the instructional responsibility for a shared group of students, there is the potential to increase student achievement.[8] In addition, teachers and schools that engage in better-quality collaboration see higher achievement gains in math and reading.[9] Team-based staffing models, when executed well, may enable better-quality collaborations. Moreover, teachers improve at faster rates when they work in schools with higher collaboration quality.[10]

What Are Team-Based Staffing Models?

At the most basic level, Next Education Workforce team-based staffing models comprise *at least* two professional educators who are responsible for a shared roster of students. In this sense, there is shared accountability and interdependence among the educators on the team. In practice, the design of every team is different, and most teams ultimately involve more than two professional educators. But they don't always start that way.

As depicted in figure 1.1, we might think about the complexity of team-based strategic school staffing models along a totally made up and wildly subjective "spiciness" scale (our models originated in Arizona, after all). Let's assume that the traditional one-teacher, one-classroom staffing model is mild (zero chili peppers). To increase the spiciness of the staffing model, we can start by simply bringing two professional educators together and allowing them to share a common roster of students. This means that both educators are responsible for the outcomes of all these students. The way that they distribute the manifold responsibilities associated with being a teacher is up to the educators and is driven by the local context and the respective expertise of both educators.

FIGURE 1.1 Chili-pepper models of team-based staffing

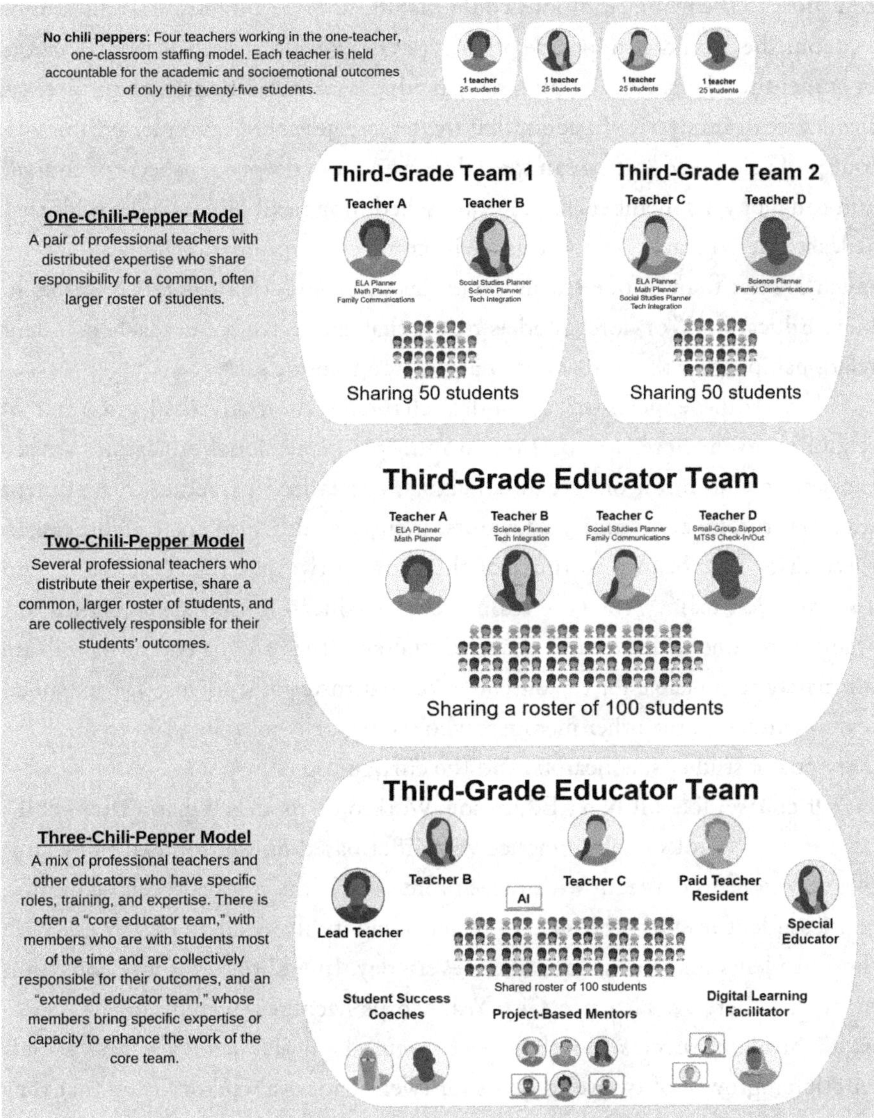

Several benefits of team-based staffing can be enjoyed at the one-chili-pepper level: the job is less isolating, educators can specialize in different aspects of it, and it is easier to group and regroup students, leading to deepened and personalized learning for all students.

Moving to a two-chili-pepper staffing model usually means adding more educators to the team. Additions could include another professional educator or two, but they could also include other types of educators, such as paraeducators or student teachers. Adding professional educators, in particular, helps increase the degree of innovative freedom that the team enjoys. For example, a team with four professional educators can specialize even more deeply in aspects of content and pedagogy, its members have greater scheduling flexibility, and the odds that at least one educator on the team will connect deeply with each student are much greater than in one-teacher, one-classroom models. In fact, educators in Next Education Workforce models report that they have better teacher-student relationships than those in traditional classroom models.[11]

Three-chili-pepper staffing models challenge the traditional grammar of schooling even more. In addition to multiple professional educators, we see the strategic addition of special educators, specialized paraeducators, student teachers, tutors, community educators, mental health workers, and others. In these cases, it is helpful to think of the team in two parts: a "core team" and an "extended team." The core team includes educators who spend significant amounts of time with the same group of students. They are the educators who are ultimately responsible for the outcomes of that roster of students. The extended team includes all the other members who strategically join the team to meet the demands of students, educators, and the curriculum.

Of course, like all Next Education Workforce models, what a three-chili-pepper model looks like in practice will differ based on the context. For example, we might find a team with three professional educators, a special educator, and a student teacher who share a roster of eighty-five students and work with those students for at least four hours every day. In addition to those core team members, there are also two City Year Corps Members serving in the capacity of Student Success Coaches, each focused on the academic and social-emotional growth of twelve students for twenty hours a week.[12] Given that they are working only with this team, and for substantial periods of time, they are also welcomed as members of the core team. The extended team might include ten family members, trained in the science of reading, who volunteer in the learning space for an hour every morning immediately following drop-off. A group of four high school students who are part of the Education Professions career and technical education program serve as math tutors three days a week.[13]

Given the team's focus on science, technology, engineering, and mathematics (STEM) this year, they have also brokered a partnership with a local engineering firm, and three engineers join as project-based mentors via video conference for an hour each week.

Although we are not currently working with any schools that have designed four-chili-pepper models, we can imagine what they might look like and know of a handful of examples currently operating. In these models, the very notion of school is different. Learning is often competency based and has multiple opportunities for student direction. Learners build their own individual teams of educators to help them meet their goals, and these educators may be formally associated with the school or not. The line between school and community is permeable and becomes more so as students increase in age or some other indication of readiness. We intentionally don't spend any more time in this book discussing four-chili-pepper models, but we do see team-based models as powerful first steps toward moving in that direction—one in which schooling is likely to move in the coming decades.

A Note: Spiciness Does Not Equal Quality

It is worth emphasizing that the spiciness of a model is not equivalent to its quality. The spiciest pepper isn't always the best pepper—the context of the food (or in this case, school) matters! The point isn't to max out the Scoville scale for heat, but rather to thoughtfully consider new ways to staff your school given your context.

Regardless of the model's spice level, we see evidence of teaming as defined by Kozlowski and Ilgen.[14] There are at least two educators who collaborate in both planning and implementation. Through shared responsibility for students' outcomes, they possess a common goal and employ their specific expertise to help meet that goal. Their roles and responsibilities differ as a function of their interest and effectiveness, creating conditions of interdependence. Together, these factors make Next Education Workforce strategic school staffing models true teams.

FOUR SHIFTS ASSOCIATED WITH IMPLEMENTING TEAM-BASED STAFFING

Once a school moves to a team-based staffing model, other shifts naturally occur. Ultimately, teams enable shifts to be made that were either challenging or impossible to implement before adopting a team-based approach to staffing. Specifically, teams enable schools and school systems to shift (1) educator working conditions, (2) what teaching and learning look like, (3) the quality of relationships, and (4) how educators enter the profession and progress in their careers.

1. Shifts in Educator Working Conditions

Number of professional educators. When moving to a team-based approach to staffing, the most obvious shifts relate to working conditions. Most notably, educators are no longer working in isolation. Instead, at least one other educator (and in most cases, many more) share responsibility for a set of learners. As described previously, the complexity or spiciness of the model reflects how many educators are part of the team, how many of those educators are around all the time (the core team), and how many come into the learning environment as needed (the extended team).

Class size ratios. With educators flexing in and out of the learning environment and students regrouping much more frequently, the traditional notion of a teacher-to-student ratio becomes very challenging. In a one-teacher, one-classroom model, class size ratios are fixed. For example, one person is responsible for the learning of twenty-five students (25:1). Maybe there is a push-in special educator or a teaching assistant, but for all practical (and reporting) purposes, the ratio never changes.

Now imagine a learning environment with one hundred students and four professional teachers on the core educator team. Sometimes all the students are together with all four educators (100:4). Sometimes a single teacher might teach forty students at once (40:1), while forty students are distributed among the other three educators (with ratios of 20:1, 10:1, and 10:1), and a push-in paraeducator supervises the other twenty students working on computers in the same learning space as one of the professional educators with the smallest group (so really, 30:1, or 30:2 if we are counting the paraeducator). The details change, but the larger point remains: class size ratio becomes much more dynamic in team-based models, changing throughout the day to better meet the needs of students. This flexibility allows more personalized and effective instruction, adapting to the varying demands of different learning activities.

Responsibilities. As the class size ratio example implies, team-based staffing models also change what educators need to be experts in, with implications for educator roles and the interdependence of team members. Indeed, many educational researchers, policymakers, and thought leaders have written about the need for the role of the teacher to shift away from a monolithic set of responsibilities and be redesigned.[15] Next Education Workforce models create the structure for a variety of educator roles and responsibilities beyond the traditionally staffed teacher.

In team-based models, it is possible for educators to specialize in aspects of the work. In an elementary model, for example, a single educator on a team takes responsibility for planning the math block. It is possible that all the educators on the team also teach math, but one person is responsible for planning the math lessons, introducing new material, and drawing up the right small groups based on the data. Another educator might take the lead on all family communication for the team, and a third might take responsibility for mentoring a first-year teacher on the team. Clearly, each would have many more responsibilities, but this is an example of how their roles and responsibilities might derive from their distributed expertise and areas of passion or interest.

The same would be true at the secondary level, with the expectation that secondary educators likely retain their content focus. It wouldn't make sense for an English teacher to run a biology lab, but one could imagine an interdisciplinary project across the two subjects and students having the opportunity to seek out either educator during project-based learning time. There is a clear shift toward educator interdependence in team-based staffing models.

Planning time and when educators collaborate. In traditional staffing models, planning time is typically scheduled at the individual level. Typically, teachers are allotted limited time outside their instructional hours for lesson preparation, grading, and administrative tasks. Structurally, without a shared roster of students or shared, common instructional time, it is challenging to codesign lessons, share strategies, and adapt instruction based on student needs. In team-based models, educator teams have both individual and shared team planning time that enables the shared instructional time to be used effectively.

Another additional constraint in traditional staffing models is that collaboration among educators traditionally occurs outside instructional time through meetings, professional learning sessions, or informal exchanges before or after school. This type of collaboration, while valuable, limits the potential for the real-time instructional support that educators might be able to offer one another that can directly enhance student learning. Team-based staffing models, however, allow teachers to work alongside each other within instructional time. Educator teams may decide to increase their class size temporarily to enable a novice teacher, who is gaining hands-on experience, the ability to watch and instruct alongside an experienced educator and see effective practices modeled in the learning environment.

Educators' schedules. In traditional staffing models, educators' schedules are often highly inflexible. They are structured around predetermined time blocks that dictate what is taught and when. Teachers usually follow the same routine each day and are responsible for a fixed group of students with limited opportunities to adjust their schedule based on emerging needs or instructional priorities. This rigid scheduling can lead to a sense of monotony, restrict opportunities for collaborative teaching, and limit the ability to address individual student needs in real time.

Teams enable more flexible schedules that better align with the diverse needs of learners, educators, and the curriculum. In traditional one-teacher, one-classroom staffing models, there is rarely flexibility in teachers' schedules. They typically work full contracts and report to school for the same number of hours each day, five days a week, for 180 days a year. There is no such thing as flexible start times or remote working arrangements. During the pandemic, many teachers experienced, either directly or through friends and family, more flexible working schedules, making the rigidity of typical school schedules more visible.

Team-based models, especially those that involve several professional educators, allow far greater flexibility in scheduling. This is certainly true on a one-off basis—for example, a biology teacher on a ninth-grade team wants to attend the National Conference on Science Education, and the team responds by offering three classes instead of four, for longer blocks of time, with larger classes. In this case, no substitute teacher is needed, and students keep learning in a teacher's absence. The same could be true on a recurring basis. In team-based models, it would be possible for the educator team to design a schedule in which each of four professional educators work from home one half day each month.

Clearly, guardrails need to be established, but the point is that team-based models provide increased innovative freedom in scheduling, whether on a recurring basis or for just a few hours on a given day.

Accountability. Finally, team-based models fundamentally shift accountability for student outcomes from teachers-of-record to teams-of-record. In many ways, it is this collective responsibility for a shared, common roster of students that truly defines a team. Because each teacher is ultimately responsible for all the learners, there is no such thing as "my students"; every educator has a stake in each student's growth and achievement. This shared accountability also changes the way that educators interact and plan—thinking more strategically about each team member's unique strengths and incentivizing conversations about students and how to help each one succeed.

Taken together, the shifts in educator working conditions represent the most profound and immediate changes to the grammar of schooling when team-based staffing models are implemented. We summarize each of these shifts in table 1.1.

TABLE 1.1 Shifts in working conditions moving from one-teacher, one-classroom models to Next Education Workforce team-based staffing models

		Traditional staffing models (one-teacher, one-classroom)	*Next Education Workforce team-based staffing models*
Shifts in working conditions	**Number of professional educators**	1 Isolated	2–6+ Collaborative
	Class size ratios	Constant (25:1)	Variable (100:4, 50:2, 25:1, 5:1)
	Responsibilities	Must be great at everything	Fewer tasks, deeper engagement with particular ones
	Planning time	Typically individual; sometimes collaborative	Protected planning time for team and individuals
	When educators can collaborate	During planning only; outside of instruction	During planning and instruction
	Educators' schedule	Inflexible; the same on most days	Allows for flexibility
	Accountability	For "my" roster of ~25 students	For the team's shared roster of students

2. Shifts in Teaching and Learning

Schools often find that moving to team-based staffing models highlights the need for shifts in teaching and learning. While not true in every model, the following shifts are commonly found in schools implementing team-based staffing: more learner-centered instruction, mastery-based student progress, a focus on broader student outcomes, redesigned learning spaces, and more flexible scheduling.

Instruction. Rather than being teacher-centered, siloed content delivered to the whole class, we often see instruction that is far more learner-centered (or learner-directed). In team-based staffing models, academic tasks can now be more interdisciplinary, especially at the secondary level. It is common to find two, three, or even four academic subject teachers coplanning and coteaching interdisciplinary, project-based units with authentic assessments of learning. While there are certainly instances of whole-group instruction, the power of a team-based approach comes from creating smaller, strategic groups so the right educators are with the right students at the right time.

In team-based models, educators can facilitate flexible groupings of students based on their needs. Instead of being placed into a group for the entire year, students are regrouped regularly as educators analyze data to determine where each student will benefit most at any given time. This means that one teacher might lead a small group focused on reinforcing foundational skills, another could work with students ready for more advanced challenges, and a third teacher might provide individualized support for those needing extra attention. And from week to week (or even day to day, depending on the data), their groups could change.

Student progress. Not only is the instruction more learner-centered, but so is student progress through the curriculum. For schools that have already made a shift toward competency- or mastery-based learning, moving to team-based staffing can supercharge those efforts because the educators can now more easily group and regroup students as a function of their progress through a set of learning standards. For schools that have not yet made this shift, teaming often raises the prospect of a mastery-based approach because educators are less concerned with covering content and instead are focused on who should be working with which student, given the student's understanding. For teams that choose to serve a mixed-grade-level roster of learners, the need to shift toward a mastery-based approach to learning is even more profound, given the often wider range of students' command of the content.

Student outcomes. In addition to a strong focus on the typical measures of achievement such as reading growth, standards mastery, and course grades, educators in team-based models often start measuring progress against a much broader set of student outcomes. These can be measures such as attendance, behavior, and—even more excitingly—around what many call "durable skills" or the Building Blocks for Learning, which include skills such as self-awareness, agency, and curiosity.[16] This shift toward caring about a broader set of student outcomes likely occurs, in part, because the educator team brings a broader belief about the purpose of education than any teacher working alone. This becomes even more pronounced when educator teams include specialist teachers (e.g., special educators, counselors) or community educators (e.g., representatives from business and industry, volunteer retirees) who might have even broader conceptions of what student success might look like.

Learning spaces. In addition to shifts in instruction and outcomes when moving to team-based staffing models, we see changes in the learning spaces. In traditionally staffed schools, most classroom setups look remarkably similar, with each classroom having the full set of all the things that we expect to see in schools (e.g., individual student desks, classroom libraries, and projectors). Each space looks the same because, like the teacher, it needs to service all the things that could happen in that learning space. In team-based staffing models, what might have been four individual classrooms is now considered one learning space shared by the educators and all the students. In these models, we find variation across the learning spaces. For example, sometimes one room is dedicated to flexible seating that can accommodate all the students at once for short periods of time. Other rooms allow students to work together in small groups, while others are tailored for direct instruction or individual learning.

Daily instructional schedule. Finally, one of the biggest shifts that we see is in the daily schedule. In traditional staffing models, daily schedules are often broken into relatively inflexible, short blocks of learning time, and there is rarely much variation from day to day or week to week. In Next Education Workforce team-based staffing models, variation is the norm. Each educator team is empowered to create a daily schedule that makes sense given their students, the educators, and the curriculum. For example, in a high school setting where a team of four teachers share a roster of 120 students, during a four-hour block of time, one might see any number of schedules over the course of several weeks. Sometimes it might look like a typical school, with thirty students rotating through four sixty-minute classes. Sometimes each teacher might have thirty students for four hours and then not see that group again until Friday. Sometimes two teachers might share sixty students for a two-hour block. If the biology teacher is out, the team might choose to not offer science that day, increase each class by ten students, and offer three classes for eighty minutes each. The point is that educator teams get to decide how to use the time. In fact, many of the schools implementing team-based staffing models have simply turned off their bells. Of course, teams are still accounting for instructional minutes to ensure that no aspect of the content is getting short shrift and they are in compliance with state or local requirements.

As described previously, when schools move to team-based staffing models, there are often accompanying shifts in teaching and learning and profound changes to the learning environments. We summarize each of these shifts in table 1.2. For a more visual representation of student and educator movement through various spaces at various times, see our Authors' Page.

TABLE 1.2 Shifts in teaching and learning when moving from one-teacher, one-classroom models to Next Education Workforce team-based staffing models

		Traditional staffing models (one-teacher, one-classroom)	*Next Education Workforce team-based staffing models*
Shifts in teaching and learning	**Instruction**	Teacher-centered Siloed, I/we/you, whole-class	Learner-centered Interdisciplinary Project-based Small groups
	Student progress	Seat time	Evidence of mastery
	Student outcomes	Narrow Academic	Broader Academic and holistic
	Learning space	"My" classroom Inflexible, redundant, underutilized	"Our" learning space Flexible, efficient, choice-filled
	Instructional schedule	Inflexible, shorter blocks Bell-driven	Flexible, longer blocks Educator-driven

3. Shifts in Relationships

A common concern when moving to team-based staffing models is whether relationships, especially those between students and teachers, will be affected negatively. The following shifts in relationships are commonly found in schools implementing team-based staffing models: students' access to adults, greater chances for adult-student connections, peer collaboration, family engagement, and educator-to-educator relationships.

Students' access to adults. One of the outcomes in which we are most interested relates to the relationships or connections between educators and learners. In traditional one-teacher, one-classroom models, it is often left to luck as to whether the educator and student will "click." This is true in secondary settings, but it is even more profound in elementary schools, where it is common for a child to have a sole teacher all year long. While there is undeniable power in the idealized connection between a student and a single teacher, the opposite can also be true—the nightmare of a student being stuck with a teacher with whom he or she doesn't really get along, or vice versa. In Next Education Workforce models, having a team of educators with whom students are working increases the likelihood that each child will find an educator with whom they connect. In many cases, we observe that students go to different educators on the team for different reasons. Finally, the odds of having an educator with whom a student shares significant identity markers (e.g., being a Black male) dramatically increases in team-based staffing models. This is true in all contexts, but especially in elementary settings. In addition, work by Julia Freeland Fisher and a long line of scholars point to the power of strong and weak ties, or "who you know," in increasing learners' social capital.[17] The more adults with whom students can build authentic ties, the more social capital they can accrue.[18]

Students' access to peers. In addition to building more relationships with adults, students served by team-based staffing models typically have access to a larger number of peers. Building collaborative skills with a greater diversity of peers is crucial in fostering a dynamic and inclusive learning environment. It allows students to be exposed to different perspectives, ideas, and problem-solving approaches, which enhances critical thinking and creativity. As Dylan Wiliam and Siobhán Leahy highlight, peer collaboration acts as a formative assessment strategy, activating students as learning resources for one another.[19] This not only prepares students for future collaborative work environments but also can lead to greater learning outcomes than working individually. Diverse peer collaboration helps students develop essential social and emotional skills such as empathy, communication, and conflict resolution, preparing them for the complexities of the modern workforce. Furthermore, working with a variety of peers cultivates adaptability and resilience as students learn to navigate and appreciate differences. Implementing structured peer collaboration, with clear group goals and individual accountability, ensures that every student contributes meaningfully and develops in ways essential to helping them advance in life, thereby fostering a more cohesive and productive community of learners.

Relations between families and educators. Team-based models can also foster stronger relationships between families and educators. Multiple educators working together can help reduce barriers to family engagement by offering more flexible and accessible opportunities for communication. These models also help provide a more holistic approach to addressing student needs. With educator teams, there is a greater capacity to identify and support students' academic, social, and emotional development. This collaborative effort can lead to more personalized and effective interventions, which are communicated to families in a coordinated manner. As a result, families can better understand and support their children's learning and development at home. The shift to team-based models enhances family engagement by building stronger relationships, offering flexible communication, and providing comprehensive support for students. This approach not only benefits students but also empowers families to be active partners and contributors in the educational process.

Relations between educators. Finally, team-based staffing models can help strengthen relationships between educators. Gallup's annual survey of workplace engagement includes the question, "Do you have a best friend at work?"[20] They ask this question because they have found an unambiguous correlation between answering this question affirmatively and job satisfaction and performance. This is not to say that educators don't have friends in traditional staffing models—anyone who has ever been to a "teacher happy hour" knows differently. However, team-based staffing models create opportunities for new, deeper sorts of relationships between educators. The ability of educators to build trust, share vulnerability, clarify purposes, and engage in productive conflict allows educators to take on the extraordinary challenge of collectively creating deeper and more personalized learning experiences for students. The quality of the relationships is a necessary condition to improve the effectiveness of teams and contributes to job satisfaction, feelings of belonging, and improved collective efficacy. By increasing psychological safety and genuinely leaning into the distributed expertise and cognitive diversity of the team, educators are able to reap rich rewards in the profession.

Ultimately, relationships matter. As described previously, team-based approaches to school staffing can create opportunities to strengthen relationships between students, educators, and families. We summarize each of these shifts in table 1.3.

TABLE 1.3 Shifts in relationships when moving from one-teacher, one-classroom models to Next Education Workforce team-based staffing models

		Traditional staffing models (one-teacher, one-classroom)	*Next Education Workforce team-based staffing models*
Shifts in relationships	**Students' access to adults**	Limited access to multiple adults Access to adults is driven by the schedule Often based on luck Relationship building often happens outside of class	Multiple opportunities to connect with many adults, often with student agency Better odds of finding educators with whom a student connects Relationship building is part of daily instruction
	Students' access to peers	Limited peer group Development of collaboration skills varies by teacher approach and skill	Expansive peer group Collaboration skills practiced daily in various group settings
	Family engagement	Family engagement driven primarily by one teacher with a single perspective	Family engagement driven by educator team with multiple insights Can be a united front
	Educator/educator relationships	Connections usually during break periods (e.g., lunch), at structured staff meetings, or outside of work hours	Deeply embedded in the work Team feels like a "work family"

4. Shifts in Educators' Entry, Specialization, and Advancement in Their Profession

When a school decides to design and implement Next Education Workforce team-based staffing models, they often create a fundamentally different set of conditions in which teachers enter, specialize, and advance in their profession.

Entry into the profession. Perhaps most obviously, a team-based staffing model creates a radically different way for new teachers to enter the profession. The research is clear on what first-year teachers need to thrive: induction, mentorship, and common planning time with other teachers. Rather than being an isolated teacher-of-record charged with essentially the same set of responsibilities as a veteran educator, a first-year teacher joins as a member of a team, with all the support that we know benefits early-career teachers. This person doesn't have just one mentor; everyone on the team is part of the support system. Coplanning happens weekly, or even daily. The team can help ensure that early-career teachers have modified workloads—whether that be taking some of the planning responsibilities for core academic subjects in elementary settings or some of the pedagogical expectations in secondary settings (e.g., building systems for absent students or outreach to families).

Responsibilities. For first-year teachers as well as educators much further into their careers, team-based staffing models help to ensure that all educators have a set of responsibilities commensurate with their training, experience, and strengths. In traditional staffing models, every teacher is expected to do all aspects of a complex job equally well. In elementary schools, this typically means planning for at least four different subjects every day, along with designing and executing countless systems, routines, and pedagogies. In secondary schools, the educators might have a curricular focus, but they also typically have responsibility for all the other tasks associated with the job (e.g., family communication, integrating new technology, and designing units and authentic assessments).

In team-based models, educators at both the elementary and secondary levels have the autonomy to organize themselves to maximize their team's collective strengths. What this looks like varies by context. Sometimes elementary teams deputize particular educators to take the lead on planning for specific subjects. Secondary teams may have leads for things like interdisciplinary units or family communication. The larger point is that there are very few educators who can do all aspects of teaching well—and that this is a problem with the job of teaching, *not* with the educators themselves. A team-based approach provides the space and structures to allow educators to live in their areas of strength and grow in strategic ways over time to complement the skill sets of the team. We have created a resource, the Distributed Expertise Staffing Matrix, to help team members identify their individual areas of expertise and see where additional support or professional learning may be needed.

Approaches to hiring. As hiring pools dry up and it becomes increasingly difficult to find a highly certified teacher for every classroom, school systems have routinely had to rely on less-than-ideal candidates just to ensure that every classroom is staffed. In fact, 86 percent of US public schools reported challenges with staffing for the 2023–2024 school year.[21] A team-based staffing model creates degrees of freedom around staffing. They allow conversations to shift from "We just need to find someone to cover this classroom" to "What unique skills does the team need in a new educator?" Instead of hiring the best of a less-than-ideal set of candidates, a building leader may choose the candidate who has the most complementary set of skills relative to other members of the team and who may even be an ideal educator with respect to a narrower set of responsibilities. Of course, having more sophisticated educators with deeper skill sets will almost always be preferred; however, that is not the reality that most hiring managers are experiencing. With a team-based approach to staffing, it is possible to think differently about hiring. For example, perhaps it becomes more possible to bring in two retired educators for 50 percent of the time or hire community assistants who can take on ultraspecific, time-intensive tasks that educators otherwise would be left to do (e.g., administering reading assessments or facilitating asynchronous online learning).

Personalized professional learning. Team-based staffing models also create a natural context for personalized professional learning for educators. In traditional staffing models, it is often necessary to ensure that every educator is proficient in every aspect of teaching. However, when working in teams, it is possible for educators to develop particular expertise in specific areas such as working with multilingual learners, integrating artificial intelligence (AI) into the classroom, and designing interdisciplinary units. Naturally, it would be ideal if all educators were experts at all things, but that is unrealistic. In a team-based approach, it is possible that every student would have access to at least one educator with a depth of knowledge and skill in key areas, and the team in total would have the breadth of knowledge essential to meeting the needs of all learners. Shorter and more applicable learning units along with smaller units of credentialing, endorsements, and advanced credentials help provide valuable signals in team-based staffing models and can be used when staffing educators for teams.

Educator advancement. In the same way that team-based models create a larger infrastructure for personalized professional learning, so do they create the context for educator advancement. Currently, if educators want to work directly with students in most contexts, they can be either paraeducators or certified teachers. School systems that have implemented team-based staffing models ultimately also consider career ladders and advancement pathways for educators working on teams. These could be opportunities for community educators (e.g., tutors and family volunteers) to become more formal parts of a school's educator workforce by becoming paraeducators or certified teachers, but also for certified teachers to take on more responsibility as lead teachers—educators who are responsible for the management and deployment of an educator team. When all the pieces work together, it should be clear to a person how she or he could start as a high school student tutoring in an elementary school, which would then open opportunities to be a paid specialized paraeducator (e.g., a student success coach) as an undergraduate. These experiences could accelerate this person on a path to certification, which would lead to being a professional teacher who might eventually lead an entire team. Because all these roles can be found on the same team, with clear interdependencies, it is more obvious how one role can lead to the next, which can lead to increasing responsibility and compensation.

When schools implement team-based staffing models, many of the current efforts around educator recruitment and retention make more sense. Educators are presented with a very different reality of what the first year of teaching might look like, and for many, it will be far more attractive. Once in the job, at any level, there are clear and obvious reasons for personalized professional learning and pathways to advance in the profession continually without leaving direct work with students. In short, team-based staffing structures can produce concrete shifts in how educators enter, specialize, and advance in the profession. We summarize each of these shifts in table 1.4.

CONCLUDING THOUGHTS ON TEAMS-OF-RECORD

In this chapter, we've explored the "what" of team-based staffing models. We've covered how we distinguish team-based staffing models from the one-teacher, one-classroom staffing model, including shifts in working conditions, teaching and learning, relationships, and ways for educators to enter the profession, specialize, and advance. In chapter 2, we will share the case studies of three school

TABLE 1.4 Shifts in the ways that educators enter, specialize, and advance in the profession when moving from one-teacher, one-classroom models to Next Education Workforce team-based staffing models

		Traditional staffing models (one-teacher, one-classroom)	*Next Education Workforce team-based staffing models*
Shifts in professional entrance, specialization, and advancement	**First year of teaching**	Alone Unsupported	On a team
	Responsibilities	All things	Match with level of knowledge and skill
	Approach to hiring	Filling classrooms	Strategic Based on teams' collective expertise
	Professional learning	One-size-fits all Seat time-based	Personalized and strategic Competency-based
	Advancement	Dead ends Teacher → admin	Pathways Team-level leadership

leaders who describe their "whys" of transitioning their schools to team-based staffing models. Their "whys" are situated in the context of the community, faculty and staff, and students and are the impetus for transformations to team-based staffing.

CHAPTER 2

Identifying *Why* a Team-Based Model Makes Sense in Your Context

In most traditional health-care settings, patients see multiple, disconnected specialists, leading to fragmented care. This model favors health-care system efficiency over what is best for health-care providers and patients. In contrast, the Mayo Clinic's vision for health care is a patient-centered, team-based approach.[1] Individuals receive services from multidisciplinary teams of specialists who work to build personalized treatment plans. This collaboration ensures that all aspects of a patient's health are considered, leading to comprehensive and cohesive care.

The traditional education system operates in a way similar to traditional health care. For elementary students, their ability to access the expertise of other teachers is often limited, and for secondary students, their learning experiences are often fragmented. In both models, staffing structures lead to teachers who are disconnected from one another. The way that learners and educators are organized in schools favors what is most efficient for the education system, not what is best for learners or the educators delivering learning experiences.

As detailed in chapter 1, we believe that team-based staffing models can provide working and learning conditions that are more favorable for educators and better for students. In both health-care and education settings, leaders identified problems that emerged as a result of their workforce design problems and saw team-based staffing as a promising solution that would lead to better outcomes for all those involved.

CRYSTALIZING YOUR *WHY FOR TEAMING*

We have noticed that as school leaders begin to consider implementing team-based staffing models, starting with a *why for teaming* not only accelerates the development of models by grounding all involved in a common problem (or problems) to solve, but also provides a means of marking progress. For instance, a school leader might start with wanting to improve reading or math achievement, increasing graduation rates, or strengthening student-teacher relationships, and believe that the standard one-teacher, one-classroom staffing model isn't delivering good-enough results. School leaders may also want to increase early career teacher retention, retain veteran educators, and deliver better learning experiences that align with their district's portrait of a graduate. When school leaders have a clear answer to the question of *why* a team-based approach to staffing will likely improve specific outcomes that their community cares about, they can both strengthen the commitment to this transformative work and better communicate a vision of the need for teams.

When committing to team-based staffing models, we have seen school leaders identify areas of focus that fall into one of two broad categories:

- Student experiences and outcomes
- Educator experiences and outcomes

These categories become a starting point for building key indicators of success. Importantly, as school leaders begin to build teams, they should ask themselves, "How do we know that the team-based staffing models are improving outcomes?" For example, consider a school leader who sees that their school community has higher-than-average student absenteeism rates. Such a leader might use this metric—absenteeism rates—as a reason for piloting teams, as well as a key indicator to identify whether teams are associated with positive differences in student attendance.

Consider a school leader who sees high numbers of experienced educators leaving their school as a second example. During exit interviews, such educators cite lack of advancement or leadership opportunities as their primary reason for leaving. The leader may see team-based staffing models as a way to create new leadership roles for veteran educators, and a key indicator of success might be the improved retention of experienced educators.

By crystalizing your *why*, you also specify the improvements that you believe team-based staffing can catalyze. What makes sense in your context may not work for a school leader in the next town over, or even another school leader in your own school system. Changing the way that schools are staffed changes how we plan for and deliver teaching and learning experiences. Therefore, we should not be surprised that adopting a team-based approach to strategic school staffing may have associations with improvements across a wide range of indicators. For that reason, school leaders may have more than one *why* for committing to team-based staffing.

In this chapter, we present three school leaders' *whys for teaming*. For simplicity's sake, we share just one student *why* and educator *why* for each school leader, although in reality, each leader had multiple reasons for adopting team-based staffing models. The school leader's perspective is critical because they serve as the mediator between system-level priorities and the unique strengths and needs of their school communities. School leaders carefully balance district mandates, policy shifts, and resource allocations with the realities of the students, teachers, and families in their communities. School leaders distill all the competing perspectives and create a *why for teaming* that not only adheres to broader goals but also reflects the specific needs and aspirations of their school communities.

MEASURING YOUR *WHY* THROUGH ACTION RESEARCH

Once school leaders crystallize their *why* for team-based staffing, the next step is to measure their progress toward the outcomes that they envision. Action research offers a practical and iterative framework for collecting and analyzing data, reflecting on the findings, and making informed adjustments to improve implementation. This approach ensures that school leaders remain grounded in evidence as they work to align team-based staffing with a broader vision for student and educator success.

Action Research Basics

Action research is a cyclical process of inquiry that involves practitioners investigating their own practices to improve outcomes.[2] This reflective and iterative process ensures that efforts remain grounded in evidence and aligned with the school's overarching *why* for student and educator success. The key steps include the following:

1. **Identifying a focus:** Define the key questions or outcomes that you want to investigate. For example, "How does team-based staffing influence student attendance rates in our context?" or "What patterns emerge in teacher retention and satisfaction when implementing team-based models?"
2. **Planning for data collection:** Decide what data will help you measure your outcomes. This could include:
   - Quantitative data: Attendance records, academic performance metrics, or teacher turnover rates
   - Qualitative data: Teacher and student surveys, interviews, or focus group discussions
3. **Collecting data:** Implement your plan by gathering data systematically over a set period of time. For instance, track attendance or administer surveys at regular intervals during the academic year.
4. **Analyzing data:** Look for patterns, trends, and insights in the data. For example, compare attendance rates before and after implementing team-based staffing or identify common themes from teacher feedback.
5. **Reflecting and acting:** Use the findings to assess whether the team-based model is driving the desired outcomes. For instance, share insights with your teams and leadership, celebrate successes likely associated with team-based staffing, and identify areas for improvement. Then, refine your implementation based on these reflections and begin the cycle again.

Measuring your *why* for team-based staffing is essential to ensure that your efforts are aligned with meaningful and measurable outcomes. Action research is a flexible and iterative framework for collecting and analyzing data, reflecting on progress, and making evidence-based adjustments to improve implementation. We also recommend tools like *Data Wise*, created by Kathryn Parker Boudett, Elizabeth City, and Richard Murnane from the Harvard Graduate School of Education, which offer structured protocols to help school leaders and teams collaboratively examine data, identify actionable insights, and monitor progress toward their goals.

To illustrate the power of a clear and actionable *why*, consider the stories of three school leaders who implemented team-based staffing models in their schools. Each one approached teaming with a unique lens shaped by his or her school's context, and yet all were united in their commitment to transforming outcomes for students and educators. Through their experiences, we see how crystallizing a *why* can drive meaningful change.

KRISTA ADAMS'S *WHYS*

Krista Adams was the principal of Stevenson Elementary, a preK–6 elementary school in Mesa, Arizona, from 2018–2023. When she arrived, she met the nearly seven hundred students, most of whom were Hispanic and eligible for free or reduced-price lunch, and Stevenson's forty teachers, a mix of novice and experienced educators. Quickly, Krista realized the disparities in students' academic growth and achievement and access to high-quality learning experiences at Stevenson compared to the outcomes and learning experiences of students' from higher socioeconomic areas.

When Krista visited other schools, she observed learning experiences that helped students build their agency and practice skills from her district's portrait of a graduate: collaboration, critical thinking, problem-solving, and communication.[3] When she reflected on her Stevenson students' learning experiences, she realized that they were compliance-based, offering students little voice or choice and few opportunities to bring in their background knowledge and lived experiences. The combination of historic academic achievement and the types of learning experiences that students were afforded—or not—prompted Krista to critically evaluate what needed to change at Stevenson.

In 2019, Krista was asked by her area superintendent to consider building a team-based staffing model. As she put it, "I was—to be honest—cautious at first. I wasn't sure if team-based staffing was the mechanism to get us to better learning experiences for Stevenson's students, but I was willing to try."

When the school year began, a pilot team of third-grade teachers began working together in ways that they hadn't before in their siloed classrooms. They planned together. They frequently regrouped students for instruction based on student needs and teacher expertise. And they considered ways that they could integrate more student voice and choice into instruction.

With schools navigating the challenges of COVID-era teaching at the time, these teachers were not relieved of the stress of the pandemic, but they were able to rely on one another in ways that their counterparts in traditional one-teacher, one-classroom models could not. After other teachers at Stevenson learned about their positive experiences—and how teams might reframe how they approached challenges—many of the Stevenson teachers wanted to be on teams for the 2021–2022 school year.

Krista's *Why* for Students

Krista recognized that the students at Stevenson were not receiving equitable opportunities to access just-right instruction or to develop the critical skills outlined in the district's portrait of a graduate. She observed that compliance-based teaching methods left students disengaged and unable to connect learning to their lived experiences. Krista believed that team-based staffing could create more personalized and engaging learning environments by allowing educators to regroup students based on real-time data about strengths and needs. This structure would also enable the right educator to work with the right student at the right time, ensuring that each child receives targeted instruction to accelerate growth in reading and math while fostering agency and deeper engagement. To measure the plan's progress, Krista tracked academic growth through district benchmark assessments, proficiency rates, and qualitative observations of changes in student agency, engagement, and enjoyment in learning.

Krista's *Why* for Educators

Krista saw that many teachers at Stevenson felt isolated and overwhelmed by the challenges of addressing wide-ranging student needs in siloed classrooms. The one-teacher, one-classroom staffing model made it difficult for educators to collaborate, share expertise, or access professional growth opportunities. She saw team-based staffing as a mechanism to foster a collaborative culture where teachers worked together to share responsibility for a common roster of students. This approach allowed educators to specialize in their strengths, receive peer feedback, and plan instruction together, ultimately reducing burnout and increasing satisfaction. Krista designed schedules with more planning time for teams and integrated mentoring opportunities for novice teachers within these teams. To evaluate these efforts, she monitored teacher retention rates, collected qualitative feedback on satisfaction and self-efficacy, and assessed the quality of collaborative team outputs through planning artifacts and team self-evaluation.

TRICIA DEGRAFF'S *WHYS*

Tricia DeGraff is the executive director of the Academy for Integrated Arts (AFIA), nestled in the heart of Kansas City, Missouri. Since its founding in 2012, AFIA has distinguished itself as the only arts-integrated charter school in the area, serving a diverse student population from prekindergarten through sixth grade. A majority of students identify as African American, and a significant number come from economically disadvantaged backgrounds.

AFIA's staff includes certified teachers, apprentice teachers, and arts specialists—all reflections of the community and dedicated to nurturing and expanding the minds of their 270 students. At AFIA, the arts are not just a subject; they are a way of understanding the world, offering unique perspectives and deepening the learning experience across all subjects.

Tricia's *Why* for Students

Tricia's student *why* for implementing team-based staffing at AFIA was to enhance the academic-arts integrated experience. Tricia recognized that traditional classroom models often limited opportunities for students to connect their academic learning with artistic exploration. Through a team-based model, AFIA could create an environment where students benefit from a seamless integration of academic and arts education, supported by a diverse team of educators and community educators, specifically teaching artists.

To Tricia, the inclusion of teaching artists alongside certified educators would enable students to experience enriched, interdisciplinary lessons that connect core academic subjects to creative practices—a core part of the AFIA mission. Some of the student outcomes that Tricia wanted to see as a result of team-based staffing included a deepening of students' understanding of academic content, leading to accelerated learning, while also addressing a broader set of student outcomes, including critical thinking and problem-solving and expression through the arts.

Tricia's *Why* for Educators

Tricia's educator *why* for implementing team-based staffing at AFIA was driven by the need to improve professional growth and support for AFIA's teaching staff while also complementing the pedagogical expertise with teaching artist expertise. Tricia observed that many educators, particularly novice teachers, felt isolated and overwhelmed by the demands of teaching. She wanted to create a more collaborative environment, where educators could learn from and support each other, enhancing their professional practices and job satisfaction. Tricia wanted to provide consistent mentorship and shared responsibilities among educators and to ensure that teaching was a collective effort.

In addition to supporting novice teachers, Tricia wanted to improve the educator experience for veteran teachers. This resulted in the creation of lead teacher roles, and part of their responsibility included mentoring early career and apprentice teachers. Also, the team-based approach at AFIA enabled the pedagogical expertise of teachers to be supplemented with the experiential and career expertise of teaching artists, who were community educators at AFIA.

To Tricia, teaming addresses the challenge of educator isolation, support for novice teachers, career advancement for experienced teachers, and the chance to bring individuals from outside of school into schools.

GREGORY MENDEZ'S *WHYS*

Gregory Mendez was the principal at Riverview High School, an alternative school in Mesa, Arizona. Students at Riverview faced a variety of challenges and historically have been labeled "at-risk." After a few years of Greg's leadership at Riverview, the school implemented team-based staffing as a way to provide a rigorous and relevant set of learning experiences for its students. Greg provides a reflection on what brought him to teaming:

> I noticed a number of issues divided "successful" from "unsuccessful" students. The factorylike educational environment, coupled with high-stakes testing and attention to learning in a prescribed time frame, consistently crippled students who had different interests, goals, or learned at a different pace. Further, the traditional high school one-teacher, one-classroom context exacerbated these problems. I began to ask myself, "Why does school have to be this way?"[4]

Greg's *Why* for Students

At Riverview High School, Greg was confronted with an urgent need to address chronic absenteeism, which was contributing to low engagement and poor academic performance among students labeled "at risk." He recognized that these students often lacked a strong sense of connection to school, which stemmed from Riverview's fragmented learning environments and weak relationships with educators. Greg believed team-based staffing could transform Riverview's culture by ensuring that all students had multiple caring adults invested in their success. Teams of educators could collectively monitor attendance, strengthen relationships through advisories, and engage students with high-interest projects that connected academics to their personal goals and aspirations. Greg also implemented dynamic student groupings, creating opportunities for students to work closely with peers and teachers in personalized settings. To measure the impact of team-based staffing, Greg tracked attendance rates, monitored graduation persistence, and collected qualitative feedback on their sense of belonging and connections with adults at school.

Greg's *Why* for Educators

Riverview's teachers faced low morale and high turnover, which further disrupted student learning and undermined the school's ability to build a stable, skilled workforce. Greg believed that team-based staffing could improve teacher satisfaction and retention by fostering collaboration, shared accountability, and opportunities for professional growth. He created schedules that included shared planning time and common instructional time, ensuring that all teachers were supported during difficult moments, such as student behavior challenges. Greg also emphasized leadership development within teams, allowing veteran teachers to take on lead roles, guiding instructional strategies, and mentoring newer colleagues. To evaluate success, Greg tracked retention rates; surveyed teachers on their sense of self-efficacy, workload, and professional growth opportunities; and analyzed the distribution of leadership roles among the faculty. He details the changes in self-efficacy experienced by teachers, noting that one said, "I feel like [team-based staffing] helped me grow as an educator a lot and really do much more for students."[5]

Greg's *Why for Teaming* at Skyline High School

When Greg became the principal of Skyline High School, he inherited a school grappling with declining graduation rates after COVID-19 and students who felt disengaged from their learning. Greg believed that the traditional, comprehensive high school structure, with its departmental silos and fragmented student experiences, limited both teacher collaboration and student success. Drawing on his experience at Riverview High School, he envisioned team-based staffing as the foundation for a redesign of Skyline's instructional model.

As part of a larger district initiative to create high schools with more career-connected learning, Greg built college and career academies at Skyline, embedding interdisciplinary teams of educators within each academy. This structure allowed teachers to work collaboratively both vertically, within their particular academy's career pathways, and horizontally, across grade levels, to create coherent and aligned learning experiences. By organizing teams that shared a common roster of students, Greg ensured that educators could build strong, sustained relationships with the students while coordinating instruction to meet both their academic and career-readiness goals. Teachers used shared planning time to codesign interdisciplinary projects, analyze student data, and scaffold skills that aligned with the district's portrait of a graduate. For students, this meant clearer connections between their high school education and future opportunities, ranging from postsecondary pathways to career-readiness. For teachers, this model fostered meaningful collaboration, mutual support, and a sense of shared purpose.

Greg's *why for teaming* at Skyline went beyond merely addressing graduation rates. It aimed to transform the school into a space where students and teachers alike felt empowered, connected, and driven by a clear mission.

A MENU OF POSSIBLE OUTCOMES

While research on the Next Education Workforce initiative's team-based strategic school staffing model is still unfolding, early positive outcomes point to the transformative impact of teaming for both educators and students. For schools, team-based staffing should *not* be considered just another initiative or an end unto itself. Rather, it's a strategic approach designed to *enhance* existing efforts, making them more effective, in alignment with the broader objectives already set by educational leaders. Based on our interviews with school leaders, and grounded in their schools' ecologies and cultures, tables 2.1 and 2.2 detail how school leaders we've worked with have connected team-based staffing models as a means to achieve improved outcomes for both students and educators.

Across all possible outcomes, you can (and should) also collect rich qualitative data and stories from one-on-one conversations with students, educators, and small focus groups.

TABLE 2.1 A menu of possible student outcomes associated with team-based staffing models

Outcome	*How team-based staffing models help support this outcome*	*Influence on design of the team-based staffing model and educational experiences*	*Possible direct and indirect outcome measures*
Student attendance	• Multiple educators = more eyes on and support for students • Increased likelihood of having an adult champion • Increased likelihood of having friends on team	• New role: attendance champion • Family meetings • Advisories • Interest-based groupings • Cohorts (e.g., ninth-grade academies) • High-interest and relevant projects • Educator looping or mixed-age student groups	Direct: • Average daily attendance rate • % chronically absent Indirect: • Student survey: "Caring adult at school"; "Friends at school"; "Sense of belonging"; "Enjoy coming to school"
Graduation and persistence rates	• Multiple educators supporting each student • Increased likelihood of feeling connections to adults and peers • Greater likelihood of having more career-connected learning experiences • Greater ability to differentiate instruction	• New roles: student success coaches, mentors • Remediation and extension time built into schedule • High-interest projects that show importance of a high-school degree • Integration of community educators into staffing models	Direct: • Graduation rate • Average number of credits earned Indirect: • Overall grade point average (GPA) • GPA in key courses • Course-passing rates • Student survey: "Sense of belonging"
Reading and math growth or other forms of academic success	• Strategic grouping and regrouping based on data • Team knowing and discussing individual student strengths and areas for growth • Pairing the right educator with the right student at the right time	• New roles: tutors, reading or math accelerators • Scheduling math and reading blocks to maximize extended teams (special educators, instructional coaches, community educators) • Protected time to review data and student progress as a team • Remediation and extension time built into weekly schedule	• Academic growth • % proficiency rates • Course-passing rates • % of grade-level standards mastered • GPA • Performance on demonstrations of learning • Current gradebook averages

continued

TABLE 2.1 ***continued***

Outcome	*How team-based staffing models help support this outcome*	*Influence on design of the team-based staffing model and educational experiences*	*Possible direct and indirect outcome measures*
Likelihood of reporting a caring adult at school	• Increased likelihood of each student "clicking" with an educator • Greater odds of students sharing identity markers with educators • More community educators = more chances to connect with students	• New roles: student success coaches, mentors • Advisories • Educator looping or mixed-age student groups	Direct: • Student survey: "Caring adult at school" • Student social network analyses Indirect: • Attendance rates • Student survey: "Sense of belonging"
Greater inclusion of, and better outcomes for, students with special needs	• All educators sharing collective responsibility for students with special needs • Each student benefitting from special educator expertise (e.g., Universal Design for Learning, coteaching strategies) • Increased collaboration between special and general educators	• New roles: student success coaches; specialized paraeducators • Prioritizing students with individualized education programs (IEPs) when building teams and schedules • Creating caseloads that allow special educators to embed themselves into just one team • Creating a master schedule to maximize SPED push-in across teams • Easily grouping and regrouping based on ability	Direct: • % of time in general education environments • Academic performance for students with special needs • Progress against IEP goals • % of IEPs rewritten to be more inclusive Indirect: • Attendance rates for students with special needs • Student survey: "Sense of belonging" for students with special needs

Fewer behavioral referrals	• Team handling more student behavioral challenges in the room, rather than sending students to administrators • Teams less likely to make biased decisions about consequences than individuals	• New roles: student success coaches, advisors • Creating team-based systems for how to deescalate behavior (e.g., sending students to another teammate)	Direct: • Number of referrals • Type of referrals • Parity in demographics between class and those referred Indirect: • Observations: % of students engaged • Student survey: "Caring adult at school"; "Sense of belonging"
Increased student agency or other twenty-first century skills	• More educators = easier to offer student voice and choice • The team modeling, teaching, and reinforcing specific skills	• New role: portrait of a learner champion (likely shared across teams or schools; helps teams infuse more skills into lessons) • Using team assembly and other whole-group times to reinforce larger skill development • Interdisciplinary, collaborative projects highlighting skills	Direct: • Student survey: "Sense of agency" or other scales • Growth on specific skills as measured by rubrics Indirect: • Number of key assignments on which students have authentic choice • Observations: evidence of identified skill in learning experience • Student survey: "Enjoy coming to school"

TABLE 2.2 A menu of possible educator outcomes associated with team-based staffing models

Outcome	*How team-based staffing models help support this outcome*	*Influence on design of team-based staffing model and educational experiences*	*Possible direct and indirect outcome measures*
Educator retention and satisfaction	• Increased flexibility in schedules • Shared workload and responsibility • Deeper connections to team-based colleagues • Work less isolating • Greater levels of autonomy • Educators focusing on strengths	• Educators helping to select new teammates • Empowering educators to build daily/weekly schedules • Educators identifying and leaning into areas of strength and expertise • Ensuring ample planning time • Maximizing blocks of contiguous teaching time for teams	Direct: • Retention rates • Educator survey: "Satisfaction"; "Recommend the profession" Indirect: • Educator survey: "Self-efficacy"; "Autonomy"; "Workload"; "Friend at work" • Number of leave days taken
Improved instructional practices/ evaluation scores	• Educators focusing on fewer aspects of teaching • Teaching more public—feedback coming from team • Educators more easily observing each other • Greater efficiency around instructional coaching; coach also observing and meeting with multiple educators at once	• New role: team-teaching coaches (to improve teams and instruction) • Ensuring ample planning time • Staggering team planning blocks (coaches meeting with many teams daily) • Creating systems for teams to observe each other (maybe across schools)	Direct: • Rubric-based observations: Instructional Planning Guide (IPG); effective teaching frameworks Indirect: • Student growth and achievement • Evaluation of academic tasks
Retention of early-career teachers	• Daily mentoring for novices from whole educator team • Making lower/less complex workloads for novices • Novices rarely alone during difficult or tricky moments (e.g., student discipline, difficult conversations with families)	• New roles: team-embedded teacher educators and mentors • Staffing teams with mix of novice and experienced educators • Investing in upskilling at least one teammate in supporting early-career teachers	Direct: • Retention rates Indirect: • Educator survey: "Satisfaction"; "Recommend the profession"; "Feeling supported"; "Self-efficacy" • Number of leave days taken • Analysis of responsibilities/roles of early-career teachers

Greater levels of preparedness among preservice teachers (e.g., residents, student teachers)	• Preservice teachers working with multiple educators and learning from the best of each • As members of a team, mentors do not have to be great at all aspects of the job; finding great mentors is less hard • More authentic opportunities for preservice teachers to work directly with students in less-complex teaching opportunities (e.g., small groups)	• New roles: team-embedded teacher educators and mentors • Placing preservice teachers into team-based models • Partnering with ed prep programs; creating roles on teams aligned with guaranteed skills (e.g., running reading groups) • Core teams with special educators often hosting dual-certified candidates (e.g., general and special educators)	Direct: • Placement rates • Job offer from placement school/district • Performance on preservice rubrics • Mentor teacher evaluation • Scores on teaching exams/performance assessments Indirect: • Educator survey: "Self-efficacy"; "Recommend the profession"
Leadership opportunities	• Creating "lead teacher" roles; opening new leadership opportunities; helping to diversify leadership pipelines • Educators leaning into strengths/interests and leading on various aspects of the work; allowing all educators to develop as leaders in lower-stakes ways	• New role: lead teacher • Creating specific or rotating leadership opportunities (e.g., one teacher takes the lead on family communications, another on tech integration)	Direct: • Number of lead teacher roles • Parity between the demographics of leaders and workforce • Educator survey: "Opportunities for professional growth"; "Unique skills are recognized" Indirect: • Retention of experienced teachers • Satisfaction of experienced teachers
Improved principal satisfaction/retention	• Easier to effectively distribute leadership, especially with teams that have lead teachers (e.g., twenty-four direct reports go to six lead teachers who lead four-person teams) • Teams creating a first line of support and reducing issues that have to be escalated to the principal (e.g., student behavior issues, dissatisfied parents)	• New roles: Next Education Workforce leadership coaches (support site leaders with teams) • Establishing clear points of contact between principal and each team (e.g., lead teacher) • Networking together site-level leaders to learn with and from each other; could include visits to each other's schools	Direct: • Retention rates • Leader survey: "Satisfaction"; "Recommend the role" Indirect: • Leader survey: "Self-efficacy"; "Autonomy"; "Workload" • Number of leave days taken

ECOLOGY AND SCHOOL CULTURE

Underlying the *why* for team-based, strategic school staffing models shared in this chapter by Krista, Tricia, and Greg is an understanding of their school community's ecology and school culture.[6] Conceptualized by Victoria Boyd, *ecology* includes the resources that your school has, the physical arrangements (in classrooms and the school as a whole), demographic shifts, working conditions, and the local, state, and federal policies that regulate your school. *School culture* includes the attitudes and beliefs, cultural norms, and relationships of your faculty, staff, students, families, and communities. Importantly, your school culture also includes the attitudes that these individuals hold toward change and any cultural norms that might support school improvements. Big questions include, "What does your community believe the purpose of schooling and education is?" and "What outcomes matter to your community?" The answers to these questions will play an instrumental role in crystalizing your *why* for implementing team-based staffing. As you continue to sharpen your *whys*, reflect on table 2.3 and consider what you know about your school context (and how you know it).

TABLE 2.3 Boyd's ecology and school culture factors

Ecology factors	*School culture factors*
• Resources (full-time employees, budgets) • Physical arrangement (number of classrooms, arrangement of the physical space) • Demographic shifts in your teaching staff, enrollment, and community • Working conditions experienced by your staff • Local, state, and federal policies at play in your school	• Attitudes and beliefs of your faculty, staff, parents/guardians, community, and students about the purpose of education • Cultural norms • Relationships among faculty, staff, students, families, and communities • Attitudes toward change • Current levels of trust and autonomy

CONCLUDING THOUGHTS ON CRYSTALIZING YOUR *WHY*

As you begin to think about *why* you might build teams and how they might improve outcomes for both learners and educators, starting with the ecology and school culture is a good first step. When school leaders think about team-based staffing, we often urge them to think of teams as a means to an end, not the end itself. In other words, school leaders have to posit that teams will lead to a set of better outcomes for learners, educators, or their wider community, and map out, concretely, how and *why* that could happen. Through this planning, school leaders will likely learn more about their school, staff, students, families, and communities and see a new relationship between all these in light of a new grammar of schooling.

At the end of the day, it doesn't matter how many teams school leaders build if they don't have a strong vision of how team-based staffing will bring about better outcomes and a firm grasp of the mechanisms required to ensure that teams work as intended. In the chapters to follow, we will move from the *what* and the *why* that we have described in these previous two chapters to the *how* of building your first team-based staffing model.

CHAPTER 3

Change Management for Your First Team

Hand hygiene was not a standardized practice in medicine until the mid-nineteenth century. High infection and mortality rates among patients were rampant when Ignaz Semmelweis, a Hungarian physician, connected the lack of handwashing by doctors to the mortality of patients. In 1847, Semmelweis introduced a protocol for handwashing with a chlorinated lime solution before patient examination, which led to a dramatic decrease in infection rates.[1]

Although Semmelweis saw the link between handwashing and mortality and sounded the alarm, it would be decades before the broader adoption of a handwashing protocol would become the norm. He did find a group of colleagues who supported the practice initially and generated evidence of its effectiveness, but handwashing still met with resistance from doctors who did not want to abandon their well-established practices. It would be knowledge generated later, specifically the germ theory of disease by Louis Pasteur and Joseph Lister, that would make handwashing a central act in health-care delivery, not just a practice adopted by some.

Like the novel and somewhat radical notion of handwashing in medicine, the practice of team-based staffing may find a similar initial resistance within the education field. Semmelweis's story illustrates many of the change management features that you might face as you launch your first team. You might have a strong *why for teaming* and have a coalition of supporters but still face resistance from some educators as you launch. It will likely take additional knowledge generation about the benefits of teams before it becomes something that is attractive, appealing, and compelling to those who are not initially interested. And the types of changes that you make will be a mix of specific, concrete changes to improve what already exists in your school and more complex changes that require shifts in beliefs, behaviors, and cultural norms.

Marci Lang and Richard Long, dean of academic innovation and assistant principal at Mountain View High School, respectively, offer this advice as you begin the change management process: "It's not just change management. It's change leadership. Leading change, not just managing the change that's happening, is, I think, the key. . . . We focus on the believers, and the believers will bring the 'wait and see' folks along."

In this chapter, we will use John Kotter's change management framework to explain how to approach building your first team-based staffing models and how to structure them in such a way that initial skeptics come on board and enduring change occurs.[2] A Harvard Business School professor, Kotter created the framework as an eight-step process that offers a road map for implementing significant organizational transformations. In addition, Everett Rogers's Diffusion of Innovations curve details how segments of the population are predictably more open or less open to innovation.[3] The framework provides school leaders with additional insight into the individuals whom they might choose first to join teams (e.g., innovators and early adopters) and the individuals who will be interested in the change but perhaps will not immediately participate (e.g., the late majority). Finally, we will identify the technical and adaptive changes that accompany that work of building and launching your first team and present some common questions and concerns so you can be prepared to address them as you lead this change.

KOTTER'S CHANGE MANAGEMENT FRAMEWORK

Kotter's change management framework is a seminal model in organizational development that is often employed when leading structured approaches to navigating change. For the purpose of building a pilot educator team, his framework helps school leaders create a sense of urgency, build a coalition of supportive key actors, and articulate a clear vision for the transition. Strategic communication, the removal of obstacles, and the celebration of short-term wins create a conducive environment for change that results in new practices being deeply embedded within the school's culture. Since this chapter focuses on change management for launching your first team, we do not discuss Kotter's last two steps—building on the change and anchoring the change in culture—but they will help you create more teams, so we encourage you to learn more about these steps as you scale teaming at your site.

Step 1: Create a Sense of Urgency Around a Big Opportunity

In chapter 2, we provided examples to help identify a *why for teaming*. In addition to communicating your *why* to your key actors, you must describe how educator teams present, as Kotter describes, "a big opportunity."[4] Building urgency around team-based staffing is a critical first step. Key actors should see educator teams as a concrete way to improve outcomes for both educators and students. Working in team-based models should appeal to educators' "heads and hearts."[5] Educators, staff, supervisors, board members, families, and the school community should be inspired by and invested in the outcomes of success and afraid of the associated risks if nothing is done.

Shay Quitno, a sixth-grade lead teacher at Hermosa Vista Elementary School, experienced this type of investment-building firsthand. Before her time at Hermosa Vista, Shay spent her first year teaching in a traditional one-teacher, one-classroom staffing model. She recounts the sense of urgency presented to her and the rest of the Hermosa Vista faculty when Heather Horne became her principal and made clear the opportunity before them:

> With our dual-language immersion (DLI) program, there was a large disparity between students who were in a DLI cohort and those who were not. Students within a cohort rotated between two educators, with one instructing in Spanish and one instructing in English. This led to the small group of students, not within a DLI cohort, to be confined to one classroom with one teacher. This group often had such great diversity of needs that one teacher could simply not meet (e.g., majority of the grade level's IEPs [individualized education programs], students in the Gifted and Talented program, advanced math courses, etc.). In addition, the cohorted and noncohorted students advanced grade levels together and were given very little opportunity to interact with peers. Educators like myself felt the sense of urgency: we were not able to effectively meet the diverse needs of our traditional group of learners. Additionally, being a first-year teacher of the "traditional" group of learners often felt isolating for both myself and my students. Heather presented teaming as a "big opportunity" that would allow for greater collaboration among students, as well as educators and mitigate some of the disparities between cohorted and noncohorted students.

Shay's reflection on the sense of urgency surrounding teaming sheds light on what many teachers already know: there are disparities in access and opportunity among the students in their schools, and they often feel isolated working within traditional staffing models. What educators often can't see—and what is a school leader's responsibility to provide—is a way out of this isolation and toward more equitable opportunities. Creating a sense of urgency while also presenting the big opportunity to surmount an obstacle inspires teachers and invites them to envision a path forward.

Step 2: Build a Guiding Coalition

Although everyone in your school community may be aware of your sense of urgency, they may not—and probably will not—all agree with your plan. Your guiding coalition, which Kotter describes as the "nerve center" of the change management process,[6] should include people from across the organization. This might include instructional coaches, members of a family advisory group, representation of superintendency, members from your union, and influential educators or those who will compose your first educator team.

Tom Fletcher, principal at Ronald Reagan Elementary in Yuma, Arizona, emphasized the critical role of gaining buy-in from his superintendency. "We had to ensure that our district leaders understood and supported our vision for the team-based model," he explained. "It wasn't just about getting permission; it was about having their full backing and understanding the importance of what we were trying to achieve." Tom shared how he worked closely with his district's superintendency to secure this support: "I spent a lot of time communicating the potential benefits and addressing their concerns directly. It was essential to have them on board because their endorsement gave us the credibility and resources we needed to move forward."

Superintendency was also involved in the guiding coalition, which empowered Tom to feel that the pilot program had the necessary support from the highest levels of the school system. This involvement also facilitated continuous communication and alignment with district policies and goals and enabled smoother and more effective implementation. "Their buy-in was a game-changer," he noted, "It showed the entire school community that this wasn't just a passing idea but a strategic initiative backed by our district leaders."

Importantly, Tom also included the voices of teachers in his school in his guiding coalition and ensured that their concerns and hopes were included in the initial conversations.

Step 3: Form a Strategic Vision and Initiatives

The strategic vision and initiatives are a set of concrete and interrelated activities that result in the vision becoming a reality. In this step, school leaders and their guiding coalitions convene to design what the pilot educator team will look like. At this point, it is important to explain how the future will be distinct from the past while discussing how to make the future a reality.[7] This includes designing and building a model that aligns with the team-based Elements of Next Education Workforce models.

At many schools, this step is led by the guiding coalition in an effort to define and refine the big opportunity of teaming and tailor the initiative for a given context. At Mountain View High School in Mesa, Arizona, school leaders organized workshops and information sessions for faculty, staff, families, and community members. They used data and research to emphasize the benefits of the proposed new approach. As a result, school leaders designed educator teams with features such as common planning time and shared student rosters. These features enabled educator teams to deliver on the types of learning experiences valued by the community.

Step 4: Enlist a Volunteer Army

Your "volunteer army" includes the people who are won over by your rationale for teaming and now feel motivated to join the movement. Kotter cautions against the idea that you need everyone in an organization on board from the start in order to build momentum. Your volunteer army will likely include the educators who will comprise your pilot team, and as we will discuss later in this chapter, it will be made up of the innovators and early adopters along Roger's Diffusion of Innovations curve.

Principal Fletcher built his volunteer army through personal invitation, tapping on the shoulders of innovative educators who he thought would be interested in team-based staffing. Tom invited his volunteer army to attend professional learning on educator teams, which happened over the summer before the pilot launched so teachers had ample time and space to reflect and design. As you are considering your volunteer army, take Tom's advice:

> We chose to start in sixth grade because we knew the teachers had the energy and that they were really open to change. They were willing to try new things. If it hadn't been for that original group of teachers, I don't think teams would have been successful. I recommend being very thoughtful about personally inviting teachers who you know will be on board, who believe in the work, who want to change, and who are willing to change.

Step 5: Enable Action by Removing Barriers

Your educator teams will likely perceive and encounter barriers that may prevent implementing team-based models. For example, if the master schedule does not enable teams to meet for collaborative planning time, they will not be able to determine how to group and regroup students throughout the day. Once these barriers are identified, your role is to mitigate or eliminate these barriers, craft policies that support teams, empower educators through professional learning, and reallocate resources. Chapters 5, 6, and 7 focus on common barriers such as schedules, space, and infrastructure.

At Aprende Middle School, Principal Renee Kory uncovered and removed barriers to implementation. One of the most significant barriers was the current structure of the master schedule. Ensuring that teachers had protected time to plan and collaborate daily was determined in strategic visioning and initiative planning. As a result, the master schedule was built *around* the requirement for daily, collaborative planning time instead of planning time being treated as an optional add-on. Renee shares, "From the very beginning, a nonnegotiable was that we were going to ensure that teams had protected time together to plan. So they had an hour-and-a-half block in the middle of the day where everybody on the entire team had prep and plan time."

Step 6: Generate Short-Term Wins

Short-term wins are a way to help your school build momentum toward team-based staffing models. These wins may be established by the guiding coalition or members of the volunteer army. Celebrating early successes should be a public endeavor. These short-term wins can be both qualitative and quantitative, empirical and anecdotal, and they are even more powerful when aligned with the outcomes associated with your *why for teams*. Educators on teams might share stories of improved student engagement, student achievement, or the personal or professional benefits that they feel when collaborating. These short-term wins can reinforce the benefits of educator teams by creating a positive feedback loop.

As Mountain View High School's educator teams began to launch, Cathy Beaudoin, an assistant principal, and her fellow school leaders noticed an immediate improvement in student behavior and engagement. These positive changes were shared with parents and the school community, reinforcing the benefits of the team-based approach and helping to build a supportive environment for further implementation. Celebrating these wins publicly created a positive feedback loop that energized both educators and students, paving the way to continued success.

TECHNICAL AND ADAPTIVE CHANGE

While Kotter's framework offers a road map for building your pilot team, understanding the *nature* of the changes being implemented is equally crucial. One effective way to categorize these changes is through the lens of technical versus adaptive change, a concept introduced by Ronald Heifetz from the Harvard Kennedy School.[8] Identifying whether a proposed change will be technical or adaptive helps school leaders anticipate the challenges that they might face and tailor their strategies according to their nature.

Technical change can be thought of as change that "can be solved applying existing know-how and the organization's current problem-solving processes."[9] Adaptive change, on the other hand, demands solutions that require *individuals* to change their belief systems, values, or behaviors.[10] As Ronald Heifetz and Marty Linsky, both from the Harvard Kennedy School, note in their article in the *Harvard Business Review*, "Responding to an adaptive challenge with a technical fix may have some short-term appeal. But to make real progress, sooner or later those who lead must ask themselves and the people in the organization to face a set of deeper issues—and to accept a solution that may require turning part or all of the organization upside down."[11]

Technical Change

School leaders often implement technical solutions that may seem effective on the surface but don't address the underlying complexities of a given problem. For instance, when student behavior concerns increase, a school leader may turn to technical change, such as implementing a new behavior management system.

This is a known solution to the problem. Teachers receive training on the new procedures, are provided with detailed guidelines, and perhaps even have additional support staff assigned to monitor hallways and common spaces. Likewise, a school leader might move a teacher the next year to the challenging-behavior class, hoping that their strong classroom management will support those students (and maybe sweetens the deal by offering the teacher a choice in prep time). In both situations, teachers are accustomed to these changes, and they may even expect them as a normative feature of working in a school. Although this quick-fix of professional learning or the movement of a highly effective teacher may seem appealing, it is a technical solution to an adaptive problem. While this may seem initially appealing, this technical solution likely will not fundamentally address the deeper issue that you are working to solve.

Adaptive Change

Shifts to standards- or competency-based grading, substantial changes to scheduling, or changes to expectations around the role of collaboration and interdisciplinarity are all ambiguous yet illustrative examples of adaptive change. What makes changes adaptive rather than technical is that they are complex and require altering one's fundamental beliefs. These changes require actors at the school to address complex problems—in this instance, accurately assessing student learning or breaking down the traditional subject-area barriers to learning experiences. Teachers may also need to change their beliefs about the purpose of schooling and the practices that they use with students each day.

As we've seen it, team-based staffing models require both technical and adaptive change to some of the most fundamental parts of schools and schooling for teachers, families, and the community. Discerning whether a particular change will be technical or adaptive is a critical task that you should perform continually as you build your first team. Without doing this, you run the risk of improperly identifying and implementing a change that has the potential to derail your efforts to build your team before you even begin.

ROGERS'S DIFFUSION OF INNOVATIONS CURVE

Making the transition to team-based models is a fundamental shift in how schools operate. As shared earlier, we recommend that school leaders seed new ideas with those who are most ready and willing to accept, and even embrace, substantive change. Carrie Furedy, associate superintendent of Kyrene School District, notes that the biggest lessons learned from launching their first team-based model was to have "teachers who are bought into the idea of teaming that you are pushing forward." In this section, we will use Rogers's Diffusion of Innovations Curve to guide your thinking about whom you should initially recruit to join your guiding coalition and volunteer army.[12]

In 1962, Everett Rogers proposed a way to classify adopters of an innovation in a form that is now known as the Rogers's Diffusion of Innovations Curve. He characterized five categories of adopters of new ideas: innovators, early adopters, early majority, late majority, and laggards.[13] Knowing precisely which category people fall into is less important than understanding the overall concept: it's important to start with the right people when introducing and scaling an innovation.

On average, innovators comprise a very small percentage of the population (about 2 percent), and early adopters comprise a larger percentage (about 14 percent).[14] One could speculate that given the compliance-driven education reforms of recent decades, innovative educators who fall on the left side of the curve have exited the profession altogether—or perhaps they never entered it in the first place—and as a result, the distribution of educators overall may skew to the right. For the purposes of this book, however, we'll assume that the population of educators in schools mirrors the overall distribution of the population, as described by Rogers and as represented in figure 3.1. On the whole, educators who demonstrate characteristics of innovators and early adopters will be more

FIGURE 3.1 Rogers's Diffusion of Innovations Curve: Percentages of a population that fall into particular categories aligned to the propensity to adopt or resist an innovation

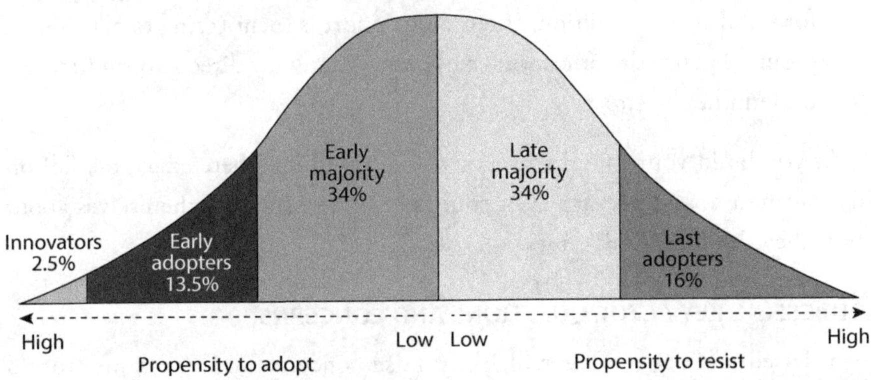

Source: Adapted from Pnautilus, "Diffusion of Innovation," Wikimedia Commons, July 14, 2011, https://commons.wikimedia.org/wiki/File:DiffusionOfInnovation.png#metadata.

willing to take risks and work productively through the early stages of launching team-based models.

Each of the groups on the Diffusion of Innovations Curve has different strengths, and each needs a different type of support. Perhaps some of these characteristics will resonate as you reflect on your own dispositions and those of the educators on your campus:

- **Innovators:** Innovators are often dissatisfied with the status quo and are not discouraged by failure. They crave the freedom to try new things and like being the first to try an innovation. Innovators may struggle to communicate the idea to others because it just makes sense to them.
- **Early adopters:** Often formal or informal leaders, early adopters are willing to take risks and want to make circumstances better for those around them. They are motivated by others who share in the vision or innovation. This group often holds a higher degree of social status and influence than innovators.
- **Early majority:** Generally positive and open to learning about new ideas, those in the early majority often need evidence of early success and are motivated, in part, by the desire not to be left behind.
- **Late majority:** Resistant to innovation, the late majority group is influenced by traditional values and practices. Those in the late majority may want to see a complete outcome before committing and need to see an innovation as the "new normal."
- **Last adopters:**[15] Highly resistant to innovation and change, last adopters are driven to maintain their current reality and hold a distinct preference for stability and tradition. If too much effort is spent trying to get this group to adopt the innovation early, the group may directly or indirectly undermine the effort.

As you build your initial educator teams, consider where educators fall on this continuum, and perhaps even consider asking educators themselves about where they think they fall on it.

ADDRESSING KEY ACTOR QUESTIONS AND CONCERNS

Team-based staffing models will likely raise concerns and questions from a variety of audiences. Identifying where there might be points of support and resistance and how to overcome resistance can be a helpful exercise, and we present a few of them here.

Inviting and Engaging Educators

Educators are at the crux of our schooling experience. It's essential to provide them with the right set of experiences early and frequently. As one educator noted early when building team-based staffing models, "I think there is a need for change [in the US education system], but I'm not sure if this [team-based staffing] model is feasible." The right set of experiences that invites and engages educators to talk about the perceived benefits and to unearth their perceived constraints will pay dividends in the long run when implementing team-based staffing models.

Common teacher concerns and resistance. There are a variety of concerns that may arise as teachers are exposed to team-based staffing models. The concerns of teachers are important to acknowledge and valid, given that it is the school staff who are asked to enact—and sometimes endure—myriad school reform efforts that have taken place over the past decades. We believe that it is important that school leaders provide time for educators to discuss these concerns and invite teachers to codesign solutions for them.

One concern that we often hear, especially at the secondary level, is about content areas and interdisciplinary teaching. One teacher identified that "other teachers seem really resistant to working in an interdisciplinary way. They want to work with the teachers that teach the same grade and same subject rather than work as a teacher unit that talks about beneficial practices that would directly impact the students who we all see." We have indeed heard similar sentiments from teachers who are building models. One said, "Not sure [that this model will work]. I guess that social studies is, by its nature, fundamentally different from the other subjects, as is every subject." Given that team-based models prompt teachers to think differently about the way that these subjects have been delivered for decades, we understand their concerns.

Another common concern centers on the shift from individual autonomy to shared responsibility and collective autonomy, which can feel unsettling as some teachers express a concern that they will have less control over classroom decisions or instructional approaches. Similarly, teachers worry about how their evaluations—which have typically been at the individual level—will change in a team-based model. Recognizing these concerns, school leaders should create active avenues for open dialogue to not only surface these concerns but also embrace educator ideas for overcoming them.

Ways to explore the elements of educator teams. There are some exploratory experiences that can help teachers as your school builds its first team. These experiences will also be beneficial for those who are part of your guiding coalition or your volunteer army, especially since all eyes will likely be on your first team:

- **See team-based staffing models in action:** To visualize success in their own contexts, educators first need positive mental models of what Next Education Workforce models look like in action. To support this need, several school systems that are part of a national network of Next Education Workforce sites host in-person site visits for those who want to see team-based models in person. We also have created a virtual, asynchronous site visit for those who want to access a guided video experience on demand. You'll find links to our in-person and virtual site visit offerings on our Authors' Page.
- **Dialoguing about the Elements of the Next Education Workforce:** At Skyline High, educators were given time to grapple with the Elements of Next Education Workforce models and consider what implementation could look like in their own contexts. Skyline took time during its weekly schoolwide professional learning block, in the year before piloting, for educators to read about team-based staffing models and to raise questions and concerns about them. Educators were able to ask questions of school leadership and were asked to consider what aspects of these models could have the most positive impact in the Skyline context.
- **Supported, low-stakes opportunities to experiment:** At Westwood High School, Principal Chris Gilmore invited teachers to try team teaching by preparing an interdisciplinary unit for a shared group of students. This enabled teachers to pilot aspects of educator teams without fully committing to a model for a whole school year. These are low-stakes opportunities for teachers to build their knowledge of and try teaming.

Communities and families. Generating buy-in from families, parents, and guardians can strengthen the initial team-based staffing pilots while also ensuring that the models are responsive to the community. As Assistant Principal Beaudoin puts it:

> A major piece of our work to build teams started with our school improvement advisory committee and talking to them about the research, past pilots that have been done, or some other instructional or staffing tinkerings here or there. Without the input of the community and families, and even community members who don't have children at our school, we could not have built teams.

Communication Strategies for Families and the Larger Community

"Transparent" and "consistent" are the two adjectives we would use to describe the type of communication that key actors want to receive about team-based staffing models. When Patty Christie was implementing a teaming model at Rhodes Junior High School, one of her key strategies was maintaining open lines of communication with her families and community. As Patty noted, "there were lots of critical eyes on Rhodes because of teaming. Many parents and the community didn't understand it." Regular communication describing the changes was a vital part of launching Rhodes's team-based model. Our school partners use multiple channels to communicate these changes to the community.

Websites. Many schools that we partner with have a specific section of their website dedicated to describing team-based staffing models. If they don't have a specific section, they often discuss their innovative work in an "About Our School" section. For instance, Stevenson Elementary says on its school website: "Stevenson employs a model of education where we have teams of educators that focus around students to provide deeper and personalized learning. Stevenson provides students with dynamic classroom environments where the classrooms are joined together and the adults move throughout the space all day long."

Social media. Social media is another platform that can support communication about the model, including photos, videos, and key takeaways. Here are some sample posts that communicate the big ideas of team-based staffing models in a digestible way:

- Imagine having a team of teachers, each with their own strengths, all helping your child. That's what team-based staffing is all about. Instead of one teacher, your child gets a whole team!

- With team-based staffing, multiple teachers work together so your child gets more attention and support. Multiple teachers working together means having a whole team supporting your kid!
- Your child deserves the best, and that's why they'll have a team of expert teachers! Each teacher brings something special to the table, helping your child in ways one teacher alone can't.
- Think high school teachers don't collaborate? Not in our 9th-grade teams! Our educators work together to support every student, ensuring a more connected and personalized learning experience.

Media outlets. As you transition to team-based models, you might consider reaching out to describe your new staffing model to news and other media outlets. These media outlets can help you communicate the changes to a wider audience of community members and provide an opportunity to address misconceptions about the model or how it differs from other similar models being implemented in your community. Examples of how news outlets have covered Next Education Workforce efforts are available on our Authors' Page.

CONCLUDING THOUGHTS ON CHANGE MANAGEMENT

Change management is an intricate and complicated process. Purposeful planning, clear communication, and initial support from multiple key actors—from superintendency to the community—will supercharge your educator teams. Constantly evaluating the types of changes that you are making—technical or adaptive—and where you are in the change process, whether you use Kotter's framework or another one, will help maintain your progress and inform your next decisions. In chapter 4, we will delve into how to build your first team after building the right buy-in to move forward.

CHAPTER 4

Building Your First Team

Apple was not always the thriving technology company that it is today. In 1997, more than twenty years after its launch, it faced several challenges: lower stock prices, significant financial losses, and a demoralized workforce. Steve Jobs returned to Apple that year to revive the company, and he began by building the right team to envision a new future and to take bold risks to achieve it.[1]

Jobs tapped multiple people with balanced, distributed expertise. Jony Ive brought design thinking. Tim Cook streamlined manufacturing and supply chain. Phil Schiller led marketing efforts. Avie Tevanian built pioneering software. Jonathan Rubinstein built cutting-edge hardware. This team's remarkable work led to the creation of notable Apple products like the iMac, iPod, iPhone, and iPad.

Perhaps you are facing challenges in your school similar to those Jobs faced upon his return. Student attendance rates might be perennially below the state average, or perhaps staff morale is at an all-time low. Or maybe you have enjoyed years of solid growth and achievement and are looking to make the next big leap. Jobs was intentional in how he selected the team that would lead Apple into its next era, and you will also need to be intentional in how you select your first educator team. The educators you select don't necessarily have to be the most experienced; what matters is that the team believes in a shared vision, is willing to take risks, and has the skills and support to succeed.

After getting clear on their *why for teaming*, many of our school partners then start asking what kind of team-based models will help deliver those outcomes and who are the right, most eager, and most willing educators to join the first team at their schools. Even if many of your first educators will be your most enthusiastic, they should be given the chance to grapple with the big ideas of team-based staffing before implementation because most of us have attended, and been trained as educators in, traditional one-teacher, one-classroom models.

Teachers need time to learn—and unlearn—what it means for a team of educators to teach a shared roster of students. To build this schema, school leaders should take similar actions as they do with those who initially offer resistance. This includes seeing team-based models in action, exploring and internalizing the Elements of Next Education Workforce models, and considering how the Elements should be applied in their particular school context. The schools spotlighted at site visits showcased by the Next Education Workforce initiative provide examples rather than blueprints, and they can inspire educators to build new mental models for what teaching and learning can look like.

For schools that are ready to move to preparing for the launch of team-based models, we recommend starting your planning process by revisiting your *why for teaming*, identifying the shared roster of students, and then building the educator team that will best support them.

BUILDING A TEAM

As you build your first educator team, you will likely toggle among three key considerations:

- Your *why for teaming*
- The students that the team will support
- The educators whom you want to include on the team

Your *Why for Teaming*

Your *why* should be explicitly tied to the decisions that you make about the students who will be supported and the team of educators who will support them. This tether will also ensure that you can measure the success of teaming in supporting your why. In addition, when communicated with and understood by team members, your *why for teaming* can drive instructional decisions that better meet the needs of the learners *and* accomplish larger school or district goals.

Consider the why for Westwood High School. Vatricia Harris was an English teacher at Westwood in 2018. "Our principal at the time knew that we couldn't keep doing what we were doing," Harris says. "We were losing too many kids. Our graduation rate was down at 68–70 percent, and we were failing too many students." The principal at the time and his administrative team examined data and noted that many incoming ninth graders had failed two or more classes in junior high. Knowing the correlation between ninth-grade passing rates and the likelihood of high school graduation, the school leadership team decided to build educator teams around their most vulnerable learners.

Because Westwood wanted to bolster students' pass rates in their core classes, the educator teams included core subject areas: English, math, and biology. The first educator teams—three teams in the first year—each shared eighty to ninety ninth graders. The shared roster included learners who might be considered more vulnerable given their junior high experience, including those with poor attendance and those who struggled academically, socially, or emotionally. The leadership team strategically invited educators who were willing—and able—to rise to the challenge of teaming, and they were given autonomy to make decisions that were right for their learners. Student passing rates increased. What the school leadership team did not anticipate was the benefit for educators as well, and that became part of their *why* for building teams over time.

The Shared Roster of Students

One of the defining team-level elements of Next Education Workforce models is that the educator team shares *one* roster of students. While part of moving to a shared roster is infrastructural, the other part of the change is the mindset shift that educators must make. As part of the mindset shift, teachers must see the roster of students and think, "These are *our* students. *We* share responsibility for the outcomes and learning experiences of *all* these students." Heather Horne, the principal of Hermosa Vista Elementary School, attests to the positive attributes of a shared roster—both in practice and in mindset—saying, "The shared roster has created a sense of community and belonging among teachers, and the competitive nature that existed on campus among teachers is far less palpable."

As part of the technical shift, it is important that official student rosters reflect the actual students that the team serves, if possible. In our experience, we have observed that when each teacher sees only a subset of students on the roster, even when the teachers are asked to work together on a team, it is too easy to default to the usual grammar of schooling: these are *my* students, and those are *your* students. Creating a shared roster of students—in hearts and on paper—is an essential first step in creating your first team.

The number of learners that the team will support. A good first question to ask is, "How many students will be supported by the educator team?" Some schools start with small educator teams comprising two certified teachers who share fifty to sixty students. This approach may make sense in an elementary school with two teachers in each grade level or a secondary school with two content-area teachers (e.g., English language arts and social studies). The small team structure allows a pair of educators to work closely together to plan interdisciplinary units, align classroom procedures and expectations, build systems for flexibly grouping and regrouping students using data, and distribute their expertise.

Other schools create larger shared rosters of 100–120 students, supported by four or more certified teachers. Larger rosters of students provide more opportunities and flexibility for educator teams. With more educators, a team will likely have increased knowledge, skills, and expertise to distribute. Also, because the teams include more adults, larger rosters of students typically provide increased opportunity and flexibility for grouping and regrouping students using formative data and increased likelihood of strong relationships.

Very large teams serving more than 150 students, however, may not be ideal, particularly in the early phases of launching team-based models. From a technical perspective, larger educator teams are more logistically complex for a school leader to organize. From an adaptive perspective, starting with a team with many different personalities and opinions can be more challenging than starting small. From both the educators' and the students' perspectives, we want their first teaming experience to feel cohesive and well organized.

So what's the high end of the range of the number of students that one educator team can effectively support? In elementary settings, we typically recommend a maximum roster of about 120 students, and many of our partners land closer to seventy to ninety. For the educator teams who support our youngest learners (PK–1), perhaps those roster numbers can and should be a little bit lower, although we have seen a kindergarten team beautifully support 100+ students.

In the secondary context, educator teams often share up to 150 students. This shared roster size roughly equates to the number of students that a junior high or high school content-area teacher would see on a traditional school day. The difference is that the educator team will share one roster of students *during the same block of time*, which creates numerous opportunities for interdisciplinary collaboration, flexibility in the daily schedule, and ability for specialization (e.g., one educator might be the lead on family communication for the team).

Your most vulnerable learners. As you consider which students will be on your first educator team, we urge you to consider how teaming might be a structure that supports meeting the strengths and needs of your most vulnerable and marginalized students: those with disabilities, socioeconomic barriers, and multilingual learners, just to name a few. While Westwood High School administrators saw increases in ninth-grade passing rates for students supported by teams in that first year, they also recognized that their first teams were more homogeneous than they desired. In the years since, Westwood school leaders have thoughtfully created heterogeneous student rosters with students of varied backgrounds, strengths and needs on each team.

Teaming is an opportunity to structurally provide students with access to a variety of educators, with their experiences, backgrounds, and expertise not afforded by the one-teacher, one-classroom model. As you design your teams, consider the types of support that you want your most vulnerable students to receive and the learning experiences that you want them to have. After all, *all* students benefit when we center on learners who need the most support—and *all* students can benefit even more when they have access to multiple educators with the expertise to meet their needs.

Maximizing inclusive practices for students with disabilities. For students with disabilities, one way to ensure that teams are inclusive is by evenly distributing students who receive special education services on teams. This approach can improve the dynamics of team and classroom learning, while ensuring that the least restrictive environment is being provided to students. As a general guideline, we recommend that team and class rosters should be limited to around 30 percent of students who receive special education services. When teams exceed this number, there is a greater chance of grouping students based on their perceived abilities—also known as *tracking*—which runs counter to efforts for inclusion.

Brad Thompson has studied special educators in team-based models and is a former special education teacher himself and has the following recommendations for considering students with disabilities on teams:

- **Mitigate the possibility of unintended tracking:** School leaders should prioritize the placement of students who receive special education services when building teams and developing the master schedule. Placement on teams should be intentional, with particular attention given to the needs outlined in students' individualized education programs (IEPs) and whether a team setting would be an appropriate placement for each learner.
- **Assign a special educator as a core team member:** When personnel are available, school leaders should consider assigning an education specialist (e.g., a certified special education teacher) to a single team as a core team member. Assigning an education specialist to one team, with the entirety of the education specialist's caseload included in the team's shared roster, has numerous advantages when designing inclusive learning environments. For instance, placing special educators on teams centralizes the general education teachers with whom education specialists collaborate and allows for deep, ongoing collaboration. This deep collaboration improves communication and allows more effective implementation of IEPs and the integration of specially designed instruction in the classroom.
- **Meet state legislative requirements through coteaching:** One common way to ensure that students are placed in the least restrictive environment is through *coteaching*, defined as the partnering of a general educator and a special education teacher to deliver instruction jointly. Coteaching enables students with disabilities to spend more time in the general education classroom and is a collaborative instructional structure that can be used *within* a team-based staffing model. Coteaching is best achieved when special educators and general educators have common time to plan and deliver instruction, which is why it's ideal that they are embedded members of the core team if possible.

The Educators Who Support the Shared Roster

As you are solidifying your shared roster of students, you are probably also considering the educators who will support the shared roster. This section explores three considerations related to your educators. First, what personal or organizational benefits will the team provide to educators? Next, how should you decide what types of educators you want to wrap around your shared roster of students? Finally, how does one actually staff the team-based roles?

Personal or organizational benefits for educators. One purpose of teams is to produce better outcomes for learners, but there are a variety of ways that teams also benefit educators, personally and organizationally. Consider how you will compose your first team based on the needs of—and opportunities for—educators in your context. These decisions include considering how you may provide leadership opportunities for your educators who are ready for a new challenge, how you will support novice teachers, or how you may provide more educator agency and autonomy. Here are a few examples of what these opportunities can look like in action:

- **Teacher leadership:** Perhaps you have several highly effective teachers on your campus, and your district's strategic plan emphasizes a priority for building teacher leadership. As you create your plans for launch, your context and priorities may lead you to draft a formal lead teacher job description and bring it before the governing board for approval.
- **Support for novice educators:** Perhaps your system has set a goal of improving retention of novice educators in their first three years of teaching, and you have a few very experienced certified educators. As a result, you might design teams with at least one highly effective, experienced educator and one or more novice educators on each team.
- **Meeting community demands for educators:** Perhaps your elementary school is located in a rural area with declining enrollment, you have just one teacher at each grade level, and your community values collective decision-making. This may lead you to design a smaller educator team of two certified educators and one part-time paraeducator who together hold collective decision-making responsibilities when serving a multiage group of students.

Personal and Organizational Benefits at Kyrene de las Manitas

Kyrene de las Manitas Innovation Academy is an excellent example of a teaming model that focused on the personal and organizational benefits for educators in addition to the learning experiences for students. Laura Toenjes, the current superintendent of the Kyrene School District and a former assistant superintendent in the district, recognized a need for supporting teacher leadership and novice educators. Toenjes noted, "We really wanted to hone in on how we shifted the profession for teachers . . . we wanted to reinvigorate those who were in the system and attract what the new generation was looking for in the workforce." This led to the development of new job descriptions, such as the "Teacher Executive Designer (TED)," a role that combined classroom teaching with the responsibility of leading a team of educators. The TED role was pivotal to providing leadership opportunities while keeping the best teachers in front of students. Kyrene de las Manitas also intentionally hires novice teachers for their teams as a form of onboarding. Novice teachers have the continuous support of experienced teachers in ways that they would not in a one-teacher, one-classroom model. As a result, novice educators can thrive early in their teaching careers.

Who will staff your first educator team? When we staff our initial educator teams, a new dynamic emerges. Now a team of educators needs to be able to execute all aspects of the job together. We no longer need every single person to know and be able to perform the exact same tasks and hold the exact same expertise as in a one-teacher, one-classroom model. In team-based staffing models, we acknowledge that people are different and lean into these strengths and differences. We staff for distributed expertise and consider each educator's experience, passions, strengths, and interests.

Staffing for team-based models is fundamentally anchored in this question: Who are the educators with the readiness, experience, and expertise to support these learners together? While your ideal composition in relation to readiness, experience, and expertise can be brainstormed in the abstract, we recognize that you may have individuals (or a set of individuals) in mind who already work at your school and meet your requirements. What matters most is that you know what the team of educators you need to bring to the shared roster looks like, based on the needs of the roster (not just what's convenient for the school or the educators). Here are three considerations for building your first team:

- **Readiness:** Keep Everett Rogers's Diffusion of Innovations Curve in mind when you identify the educators who will be part of the first team. Innovators and early adopters will be most able to embrace the quick iterations and learning that happen in the first year of launching team-based models.
- **Experience:** When possible, include veteran, midcareer, and novice teachers on the team. Each experience level brings a different kind of strength to the team. One lead teacher says, "As a lead teacher, my role is to help new teachers become experts in their field. I've been teaching for twenty years now, but I still learn from the newer teachers." A first-year novice teacher on the same team offers, "Being a first-year teacher on a team means I get to work with different people who give me constant feedback. I am growing five times more than I would in a traditional classroom."
- **Expertise:** Consider the strengths and passions of educators. This could include consideration for subject-area expertise, but it also might include other strengths and passions less often considered in education. For example, one educator might be particularly good at having difficult conversations with parents and families. Another educator might connect well with students on a personal level and know whole-child strategies for helping students to recenter after challenging moments. Other educators may bring personal passions such as podcasting, technology, or visual or performing arts that translate well into designing authentic, student-centered learning experiences. Lean in on those differences and build a team with varied expertise and passions.

Identifying roles on the educator team. Table 4.1 captures examples of core team roles that we've seen school partners use as part of their educator teams. Many school leaders first identify core team members, consider the additional skills and strengths needed to support the shared roster of learners, and add

TABLE 4.1 Sample roles for educators on teams

Role	*Key responsibilities*
Lead teacher	• Leads and deploys the team of educators • Facilitates team meetings • Models strong instruction and data-informed planning • Provides feedback to teammates (could be evaluative in some contexts)
Team teacher	• May lead planning and/or instruction around specific content • Takes on specific pedagogical or other responsibilities (e.g., family communication lead, mentor to student teacher, expert in classroom technology, lead planner for all project-based learning units)
Special education teacher	• Organizes the team to support all aspects of the IEP process • Supports universal design for learning integration in all lessons
Multilingual learner educator	• Ensures that the needs of all students with language needs served by the team are met • Organizes the team to support all aspects of the language acquisition process • Supports sheltered language strategy integration in all lessons
Reading specialist, academic interventionist, and other specialized assignments	• Provides targeted support for the highest-need learners in particular areas • Strategically supports individual or small group learning and assessment
Instructional assistant/paraeducator	• Strategically supports individual or small-group learning and assessment • Supports students' learning online • Recess duty or other coverages
Community educators, such as student success coaches (e.g., CityYear or Americorps members), tutors, project-based mentors	• Checks in and out with a subset of students each day • Provides academic and socioemotional support to a strategic subgroup of students
Teacher residents (with yearlong or semester-long placements)	• Strategically supports individual or small-group learning and students' learning online • Takes on increasing responsibility for aspects of planning and instruction over time

extended team members who can provide that distributed expertise. Each school determines which roles to use to meet their *why* and the needs of their learners. In table 4.1, with the exception of the lead teacher, which is always a core team role, the roles can be designed as members of the core team or the extended team.

How Will You Staff Your First Educator Team?

Once you've determined your shared roster of students and what kinds of educators you need based on that roster, you'll need to select educators for your first team. Most schools use a combination of the approaches listed here as they form their educator teams:

- **Create job descriptions:** If you are creating new, formal roles on your team that don't currently exist in your system (e.g., "lead teacher"), you will almost certainly need to create a job description. Even if you don't technically need new job descriptions (e.g., "lead teacher" is not a new role but instead a classroom teacher who will receive a "lead teacher stipend"), many school partners find that the collaborative process of creating job descriptions acts as a way to clarify the vision for the school's team-based model and create shared understanding among key actors. Drafting the job description also provides helpful clarity for the educator who takes the role. If you choose to create job descriptions, we see school partners use them in these two ways:
    - **Bring the job descriptions to your governing board for approval:** This approach makes sense if you want to offer compensation that is different from the existing roles within the system (e.g., for a lead teacher role) and you want to provide visibility for your board and ensure that structures are built into your system that will support the implementation and expansion of team-based models over time. This may also be a good approach for collaborating with partners such as unions or other school-based associations.
    - **Use the job descriptions in informal, internal hiring processes:** If you want to build educator teams using the educators you already have on campus, this may be a good approach. Candidates have an opportunity to understand the roles that they would be taking, and by moving through an application process, they have an opportunity to highlight strengths of theirs that may not be evident in a one-teacher, one-classroom role.

    In either of these approaches, the hiring process (whether formal or informal) can be tailored with interview questions and performance tasks that reflect the needs of the team and make clear to candidates what they'll be taking on in their new role. Many school leaders empower educators—members of the team, for example—to play a role in the hiring process, and this strategic move can go a long way toward building collective ownership and team culture.

- **Select a highly functioning grade-level team:** In elementary settings in particular, some school leaders select a group of educators who already work together with a strong culture and relationships. In the secondary setting, sometimes there are educators (e.g., a biology teacher and a social studies teacher) who have already worked together to plan interdisciplinary units. If needed, school leaders may move teachers to different grade levels or course assignments in order to build a team that is excited to take on the challenge of launching team-based models.

  If you choose this approach, we recommend that you keep the Diffusion of Innovations Curve in mind and prioritize hiring for mindset and a willingness to take risks and learn together. You may need to ask educators to move to different learning spaces to create the physical proximity for the team that allows dynamic grouping and regrouping of learners.

  Give yourself permission to consider what's best in the long term, as opposed to short-term change management implications. If, for example, you have an existing group of fifth-grade teachers who work well together on the whole, but you know that one of those teachers resists change (and perhaps falls into the late adopter category, see more in chapter 3), consider making a change and identify a new team member for the educator team.
- **Invite educators to opt in:** After providing educators with opportunities to explore the concept of team-based models and see examples from other schools, ask for volunteers who are interested in being the first to launch the bold idea of team-based strategic staffing in your context. Encourage educators to talk with each other and consider whether they would like to work closely together. Importantly, you'll want to assess these educators' *click factor*—their ability to "just click" with the other members of the team. Finding educators who like each other is extraordinarily helpful when building teams, especially your first team. This doesn't mean that educators have to get along all the time—because they won't. But like any healthy relationship, those in it must genuinely like and respect

each other and appreciate how they are better together. On many occasions, teammates have described their team-based colleagues using words like "work besties," "professional twins" (or triplets!), and "copilot."

Picking the Right First Team at Stevenson Elementary

Krista Adams, a former school principal who designed and implemented one of the first Next Education Workforce models at Stevenson Elementary, selected the educators who would staff her first team, a team of third-grade teachers, based on the fact that she "trusted their commitment and their desire" and she "felt like [they] could learn alongside each other." She knew that the teachers with whom she chose to work on the pilot third-grade team already had the characteristics of effective collaborators, saying, "If you were to look at these pilot teachers before they began to team, they would already meet frequently and plan together. They would look at data together. They started sharing students for different interventions. They shared resources. So these pilot teachers already really seemed to enjoy collaborating, which was helpful for the first team because it meant that they had some established relationships."

In addition to their already developed relationships, Adams identified an "eagerness to change instruction and what learning experiences for students could look like" as another characteristic that supported her decision to invite those initial teachers to pilot. These teachers were not, as Adams said, the most veteran educators. What made them an optimal first choice was that they were "just really willing to try things and learn and grow."

DETERMINING THE NUMBER OF TEAMS TO LAUNCH IN THE FIRST YEAR

Many school leaders ask: What is the ideal number of teams to launch in the first year of implementing team-based models? Starting small is helpful, given the hard work of moving away from the one-teacher, one-classroom grammar of schooling. The most successful pilots that we have seen began with one team or just a few teams per school. The decision between going with one team and a few teams often has to do with school size and how many innovative educators are invested in and eager to do the work. Some school leaders invest in starting with just one team, while others begin with multiple teams so the teams can learn from each other through the piloting process.

Educator readiness and mindset are primary considerations in determining how many teams you choose to launch. If only two or three educators on your campus fall into the innovator and early adopter categories on Rogers's Diffusion of Innovations Curve, consider whether you have an opportunity to hire educators who demonstrate an early adopter mindset. If not, in year one, you may decide to launch with just one team. However, there are advantages and disadvantages to launching just one team.

Advantages of Launching Only One Educator Team

When launching just one team, school leaders can provide more tailored support to that team, enabling more personalized guidance and resources. In addition, the team is likely to include members who are early adopters or innovators, making them well positioned to implement new practices. With fewer students involved initially, there may be less resistance from families and educators, which can simplify the change management process. Finally, starting with a single team makes it easier to address infrastructure challenges such as developing team-based systems and adjusting master schedules, creating a smoother transition to educator teams.

Disadvantages of Launching Only One Educator Team

Launching multiple teams enables school leaders to compare and contrast challenges and successes across different groups. This approach makes it less likely that the success of team-based staffing will be attributed solely to a few early adopters. Instead, it will likely highlight how specific implementation strategies influence results. As different teams experiment with varied approaches, this diversity will foster rapid iteration and collective learning. Also, educator teams can support one another, share insights, and build on each other's successes.

SUPPORTING THE LAUNCH OF YOUR EDUCATOR TEAM

As you launch your first team, you will quickly realize that there is a new and different need to support educators in their ability to work productively together. Educators will not need support in the same ways that they did in one-teacher, one-classroom staffing models. Many educators will need to reconsider their beliefs and translate those beliefs into new practices. Therefore, it's essential that we empower educator teams to try new approaches.

Focus on Team Dynamics and Culture

An important support that school leaders can give educator teams initially is permission to focus on building team culture. As Jill Loveall, an instructional coach at ASU Preparatory Academy duly notes, "You cannot spend too much time building team culture and team dynamics. Teachers will want to get right into the details, but until you have those established teams where they have trusting relationships and value everyone's voice, they won't be able to effectively solve those problems as they arise."

We have seen challenges when teams try to get right to work on teaching and learning. Working on a team is vastly different from working in isolation, and there will be conflicts and challenges that the educator team will have to learn how to handle collectively. Educators need time to transition to this new working dynamic. Our Authors' Page includes some resources and protocols to help teams build culture and discover their working styles so they can be effective teammates.

Provide Autonomy to Educator Teams

Collective autonomy for the first educator team is of the utmost importance during the initial year. The school leadership team should provide guidance—in fact, it's essential that they provide guardrails around the priorities for learners and outcomes. School leaders set the strategic vision for building and scaling team-based staffing models at their sites, including the outcomes that they want to associate with implementing a team-based approach to staffing. Within those guardrails, educator teams should be given the opportunity to try new approaches that better meet the needs and interests of their learners.

Just as this approach requires new beliefs about teaching and learning on the part of educators, you may also need to reframe your beliefs about what it looks like to work as an educator. You were likely prepared to lead a school staffed in the normative one-teacher, one-classroom model, so it's important to constantly check your own leadership biases and dispositions as you help others transition to a team-based staffing model.

The first educator teams launching in a school need to be given the opportunity to try new approaches, reflect, and adjust. Remember that innovators and early adopters need and want autonomy to try new things and will thrive in this environment. They can lay the groundwork for those who will come after them and provide an example of what is possible when a team of educators wrap around a shared roster of students.

The school leadership team needs to be ready to celebrate successes *and* embrace failures. There will be times when an educator team tries an approach and it doesn't go well—and those are some of the most powerful learning moments for teams! School leaders need to help educator teams recognize that true learning involves making mistakes, and it's OK to take risks when we use the opportunity to reflect and fail forward.

In an educational environment that often views mistakes as things to avoid, school leaders will need to intentionally create space and psychological safety for the educator teams. If we want our learners to feel safe taking intentional risks in their learning and stretch beyond what's comfortable, we need to create parallel conditions for our educators and give them the opportunity to reflect, adjust, and move forward.

CONCLUDING THOUGHTS ON BUILDING YOUR FIRST TEAM

As you prepare to launch your first educator team, remember that this process is both an exciting opportunity and a complex challenge. The careful selection of your learners and educators and the thoughtful design of teams will set the foundation for your school's ability to scale this work later. Starting small can provide tailored support and ease the transition, while launching multiple teams can accelerate learning and foster collaboration among educators.

Regardless of the size or number of teams that your school decides to launch, it's essential to create an environment where autonomy is balanced with strategic guidance. Educators need permission to innovate, take risks, and grow together. As you move forward, the next critical step will be to establish one of the key enabling conditions for these teams—the master schedule, which will be detailed in chapter 5. This will serve as the structural backbone that supports the dynamic, flexible, and collaborative work of your educator teams, ensuring that they have the time, space, and resources needed to thrive.

CHAPTER 5

Building the Master Schedule to Support Team-Based Staffing

In his book *Advice to a Young Tradesman*, Benjamin Franklin wrote that "time is money." When it comes to staffing our schools, this aphorism holds true, especially as school leaders craft their master schedule. With a set amount of full-time employees, dictated by funding and enrollment, the master schedule determines how many educators will go where, when, and for how long. The master schedule also dictates what learning experiences educators will be able to implement.

School leaders have debated how to craft the master schedule for decades.[1] Secondary schools have toggled between traditional period scheduling, with classes typically less than an hour long, and block scheduling, with classes lasting more than an hour. School leaders have been unable to escape these two scheduling options because they are the best ways to support staffing in the one-teacher, one-classroom model.

In the traditional grammar of schooling, all class periods are bounded sets of time. A secondary educator teaches the roster of students assigned to them for a specific period of time each day or week. Elementary educators may have slightly more flexibility in how much time they choose to spend on each subject each day, but guidelines and requirements for how the instructional day must be used are typically provided by school leadership. In both cases, how educators and students are matched is often a combination of randomization and maximization of available time blocks within the school's scheduling constraints. While there are some major differences in how elementary and secondary school leaders construct their schedules, there are two key similarities in terms of the impact on students and educators:

1. Educators usually do not share the *same* learners at the *same* time, which minimizes their ability to support students in strategic ways.
2. Educators' planning periods are usually scattered across the day, minimizing their ability to work collaboratively in deep and meaningful ways.

THE IMPORTANCE OF SCHEDULES FOR TEAM-BASED STAFFING

When Skyline High School began to build teams, Marta Connally, a seasoned classroom teacher, immediately recognized the importance of the master schedule. "The master schedule was crucial in allowing for common planning time and creating flexible learning environments," she said. "Without that, the whole idea of effective teaming just wouldn't work." Building a strategic master schedule is an essential step in creating the conditions for the successful launch of team-based models. A school's master schedule is the underlying foundation that enables educators to collaborate deeply with one another for purposes of codesigning and codelivering instruction for the shared roster of students.

Team-based staffing provides a newfound ability to be creative with *where* educators and students are learning, *what* they are learning, and *how* they are learning it. When constructed correctly, the master schedule enables educator teams to do the following:

- Group students dynamically
- Plan collaboratively
- Utilize extended team members, including community educators
- Deliver interdisciplinary learning experiences rather than siloed content lesson plans

We recognize that there are still state requirements for instructional minutes that may guide the use of time in elementary schools. In secondary schools, students may still need to meet the Carnegie hours—the requisite seat time hours to earn one credit—for a particular course. Throughout this chapter, we invite you to consider how your requirements can still be met with modifications to master scheduling.

ALIGNING THE SCHOOL'S PRIORITIES AND *WHY* WITH THE MASTER SCHEDULE

As shared previously, team-based staffing models are not another initiative to add to a school's plate. Rather, they are a vehicle for helping schools achieve the vision, initiatives, and/or goals that a school system already has in place. Some school systems may have a "portrait of a graduate," a district-wide framework which articulates the district's vision for teaching and learning. Other schools may have recently implemented a new math curriculum, or decided, based on input from students, families, and the community, to begin a deep focus on the arts. Whatever a school's thoughtful priorities may be, the master schedule should work to support, amplify, and enable these existing priorities, not compete with progress that schools are already making.

Returning to the *Why*

Going back to the why for team-based staffing models is an important first step when creating the master schedule. Consider the following examples:

- If a school's *why* for implementing team-based models is anchored in creating more flexible and sustainable roles for educators, the school leadership team might
  - Consider new part-time educator roles
  - Schedule electives to give educators two back-to-back prep periods for extended planning time each day
- If a school's *why* for implementing team-based models is building strong foundational literacy skills through personalized support for students, the school leadership team might
  - Schedule each team's literacy intervention blocks at different times during the school day, enabling reading specialists and literacy-focused instructional assistants to join each team as extended team members to provide more personalized support for all learners
  - Schedule weekly planning time when all core team and extended team members can review formative data and adjust student groupings and discuss instructional strategies

- If a school's *why* for implementing team-based models is to give students the opportunity to explore various career pathways with core academic content, the school leadership team might:
  - Create ninth-grade teams in which all students take a career exploration class that is flexible enough to give them a taste of all career and technical education programming at their school
  - Empower educator teams to create project-based learning experiences in which students engage with their academic and career content

By drawing on existing school priorities and the why for team-based models, whatever it is, school leadership teams—in collaboration with educators and the school community—are able to align how educators and students use their time each day with the outcomes that they most want to achieve.

MAJOR CONSIDERATIONS WHEN BUILDING THE MASTER SCHEDULE

There are three major considerations when building a master schedule to support team-based staffing:

- **Educators share the *same* students at the *same* time:** The same team of educators shares the same students at the same times throughout the day. This allows strategic grouping and regrouping of students using formative data.
- **The core educator team has a *contiguous* block of instructional time:** The same educators, teaching their shared roster of students, have a prolonged block of time to deliver instruction. This block of time can be divided in many ways at the educator team's discretion without affecting the rest of the school.
- **Educators have the *same* planning time:** The team of educators should have the same planning time so that they can coordinate and collaborate. These planning times should strike a balance between individual educator planning time and team planning time.

Elementary School Schedules

Compared to secondary schools, designing schedules that support team-based staffing models is relatively easier in elementary contexts. Most elementary educators working in traditional one-teacher, one-classroom models already have students for contiguous blocks of time. What must be solved in the master schedule is how to achieve protected planning time for the educator teams. To do this, specials—art, music, physical education, world languages—are stacked or staggered to ensure that educator teams have protected time to collaborate. We have seen schedules in which educators have one large block of coplanning time or two shorter blocks of coplanning time throughout the day. Table 5.1 depicts a sample schedule for an elementary team. Note that there are two protected planning blocks every day, and the team members can decide whether they spend time together or individually (or this might be described in a collective bargaining agreement with the local teachers' union).

TABLE 5.1 A sample elementary school schedule

Time	*Students*	*Educators*
8 a.m.	Students begin arrival	Protected planning time (team-based or individual)
8:50–9 a.m.	Morning assembly	
9–10:20 a.m.	Content learning session 1	
10:20–11:40 a.m.	Content learning session 2	
11:40 a.m.–12:35 p.m.	Specials/electives	Protected planning time (team-based or individual)
12:35–1:15 p.m.	Lunch and recess	Lunch
1:15–1:35 p.m.	Student-selected mindfulness time	
1:35–2:55 p.m.	Content learning session 3	
2:55–3:15 p.m.	Recess	Recess duty
3:15–3:47 p.m.	WIN (What I Need) Time	
3:47–3:50 p.m.	Dismissal	

Secondary School Schedules

Secondary schools typically do not have large, contiguous blocks of time shared across educators who teach the same students. In fact, many secondary school schedules are driven by boutique and low-enrollment classes. There are a variety of ways to build a schedule for a team in secondary schools, and we think about these in the context of "levels of implementation." Each level of implementation is a valid way of master scheduling teams, but the higher the scheduling level, the more ideal the configuration.

Schedule level 1: Same students at the same time. Table 5.2 illustrates a "Schedule Level 1" configuration. Schedule Level 1 configurations are characterized by teams sharing the same students at the same time, although the times are dispersed throughout the day and teachers do not share common planning time. This schedule resembles what might be traditionally known as a "house" model. In a traditional house model, the students might be shared, but not at the same time. Notice that groups A, B, and C all have the same team of teachers. Both house models and Schedule Level 1 models allow some planning of interdisciplinary units. In Schedule Level 1 models, the educators have the ability to group and regroup students across three subjects in each period in ways that are responsive to formative data, including student interest. For example, if working on an interdisciplinary project, students in period 1 could work with any of the three educators. Looking at formative data, however, is challenging in Schedule Level 1, given that teachers do not share a common planning time.

Schedule level 2: Same students at the same time, with common planning time. In Schedule Level 2 configurations, educators share the same students at the same time and also have common planning time. This ensures that educators are able to analyze formative data and make collective instructional decisions for the entire shared roster of students (see table 5.3).

TABLE 5.2 A "Schedule Level 1" master schedule where a set of educators share the same students at the same time

	Mr. Washington	*Ms. Beecher*	*Ms. Aguinaga*
1	BIO–Group A	ENG–Group B	SS–Group C
2			Planning
3	BIO–Group B	ENG–Group C	SS–Group A
4	Planning		
5	BIO–Group C	ENG–Group A	SS–Group B
6		Planning	
7			

Note: For simplicity, electives or other non-teamed courses taught by these educators are not represented.

TABLE 5.3 A "Schedule Level 2" master schedule where a set of educators share the same students at the same time and have common planning time

	Mr. Washington	*Ms. Beecher*	*Ms. Aguinaga*
1	BIO–Group A	ENG–Group B	SS–Group C
2			
3	BIO–Group B	ENG–Group C	SS–Group A
4	Planning	Planning	Planning
5	BIO–Group C	ENG–Group A	SS–Group B
6			
7			

Schedule level 3: Same students at the same time in contiguous blocks, with common planning time. While Schedule Level 2 enables teachers to make instructional decisions for the entire shared roster of students—including regrouping students—the scope of learning experiences that educators are able to deliver is limited by the short blocks of time. To maximize flexibility and the types of learning experiences that educators can implement, providing contiguous blocks of instructional time is ideal. Schedule Level 3 gives educators the opportunity to increase or decrease the duration of subject-specific lessons based on curricular needs (an extended science lab, full performance of a play) and student needs (e.g., work time on interdisciplinary projects, academic enrichment or remediation) and enables students to be grouped and regrouped easily and complete longer-term interdisciplinary projects (see table 5.4).

TABLE 5.4 A "Schedule Level 3" master schedule where a set of educators share the same students, during clustered blocks of time, with common planning time

	Mr. Washington	*Ms. Beecher*	*Ms. Aguinaga*
1	BIO–Group A	ENG–Group B	SS–Group C
2	BIO–Group B	ENG–Group C	SS–Group A
3	BIO–Group C	ENG–Group A	SS–Group B
4	Planning	Planning	Planning
5			
6			
7			

TABLE 5.5 A "Schedule Level 4" master schedule where a set of educators, with shared common planning time, share the same students during a flexible learning block

	Mr. Washington	*Ms. Beecher*	*Ms. Aguinaga*
1 2 3	Mr. Washington + Ms. Beecher + Ms. Aguinaga Groups A, B, and C Students working through BIO + ENG + SS content with playlists, mini-lessons, and educators available for one-on-one and small-group lessons (May require flexible seat-time policies or tracking of instructional minutes)		
4	Planning	Planning	Planning
5			
6			
7			

Schedule level 4: Flexible learning blocks. One final configuration is a completely flexible block of time for both educators and students (see table 5.5). In this block, students work through biology, English, and social studies content with playlists, mini-lessons, and educators available for one-on-one and small-group lessons. In this model, students' learning is untethered from instructional minutes and dependent on demonstrations of mastery and competence. A schedule such as this would enable a larger variety of electives to be available to students who would decide which they would like to attend. For instance, Introductory Band might be from 10 to 11 a.m. every day, and students who elected to take band would leave the learning block during that time. This scheduling configuration could even be utilized at the elementary level, where groups of learners leave the learning environment for electives, reducing the ratio of students to teachers and enabling more personalized learning to happen. Importantly, decisions such as these require more flexibility in building schedules and often mean a move away from seat-time based requirements.

CONSIDERATIONS FOR BUILDING A MASTER SCHEDULE THAT MAXIMIZES THE EFFECTIVENESS OF TEAMS

Shared Instructional Time Enables Dynamic Student Groupings

In team-based models, the team of educators share students at the *same time*, allowing frequent grouping and regrouping of students using formative data. We call this ongoing regrouping of students "team-enabled, dynamic student grouping." Melissa Grandigo Taylor, the principal of Kyrene de las Manitas Innovation

Academy, focuses on creating a schedule that allows dynamic student groupings, emphasizing, "The goal of our schedule is to make sure that students can be moved around to better meet their learning needs, and that teachers have the time and space to plan for these shifts through common planning time."

The science of learning and development tells us that "variability in learning is the norm, not the exception."[2] In some one-teacher, one-classroom settings, educators may group students by perceived ability in different tracks in an effort to better meet student needs. Tracking students—for example, grouping students into honors classes—can perpetuate and reinforce educational inequities.[3] Educators may do this with the best of intentions, but research tells us that students in lower tracks often have limited access to high-quality curricula and the best educators, less access to more advanced peers, and limited ability to access advanced content (or courses) later in their educational careers.

So what's a better way to meet student needs and address the wide variability among learners? Rather than tracking students, educator teams that use team-enabled dynamic student grouping are able to respond to student data and adjust student groupings frequently. In addition, educator teams can identify the educator who is best equipped to meet the needs of particular students, balancing educator experience and expertise. They can also adjust group sizes to ensure that all students have access to a more personalized learning experience.

Schedules that allow school-based educators to be easily shared among teams. Depending on the size of the school and the number of students served by single teams, it is often true that particular educators are shared across multiple teams. These may include special educators, paraeducators, and educators in other specialized roles (e.g., specific elective teachers, specialized content teachers, literacy specialists).

Identifying which educators will place the greatest constraints on the master schedule allows you to start with them and build a schedule that maximizes their ability to work across teams. Be creative and open to negotiation, especially when considering shared educators like elective teachers. Kelsey Christofferson, the principal at Stevenson Elementary School, first had conversations with her "early adopter" elective teachers about the need to find solutions that enabled common planning time for teachers. Then she spoke with her elective teachers about the drivers of the master schedule. "Building a team-based staffing model requires educators beyond the core team," Christofferson said. "For me, to create a schedule that maximized common instructional and planning time, we all have to work together towards the vision of our school. Success in the model includes everyone on campus."

Times that maximize participation from community educators. For members of the community who are not at the school full time, building schedules that maximize their ability to participate can dramatically increase their likelihood of joining the team. Specifically, beginning- and end-of-day blocks and blocks around typical lunch hours are especially good times to welcome others onto teams as community educators.

Times at the beginning and end of the day are especially convenient for family members who might already be at the school dropping off or picking up students. Early morning times are also good for people commuting to their regular day job. Stopping first at a school for thirty to sixty minutes is far less disruptive than commuting to an office and then leaving in the middle of the day. If leaving in the middle of the day is necessary, times around typical lunch hours provide added flexibility for professionals serving in community educator roles. In these cases, it is much less disruptive to join a team for thirty minutes as, say, a project-based mentor or an industry expert for a unit of study if that time runs up against a natural break like lunch. Many of these engagements happen over video conference, but in cases in which the community educator is coming into the learning space, having the buffer of a lunch break allows more travel time.

Whether creating time at the beginning, middle, or end of the day, it is important to align the block of time with the purpose of the educators joining the team. For example, let's say that project-based mentors from the community will be meeting with groups of students for an hour once a week to advise them on their work. Having that hour coincide with a dedicated and protected project-based learning time on the calendar *and* either at the beginning of the school day or around a standard lunch hour may help increase the likelihood of recruiting mentors.

Times aligned to other known schedules. Knowing one's context is critical when building a master schedule that allows particular educators to join the team at particular times. For example, if one were looking to build a partnership with a local high school where aspiring teachers enrolled in an education professions class were trained in literacy skills and came into a neighboring elementary school as reading tutors, it would be essential to ensure that the reading block for the elementary team(s) aligned with the time of the education professions class at the local high school.

WAYS TO ADD MORE FLEXIBILITY WHEN BUILDING SCHEDULES

There are several concrete ways to add flexibility to schedules. Mixed-age offerings, using community educators, and virtual electives are just some of the ways that school leaders can build master schedules that accommodate team-based staffing models. In addition to these ideas, we now describe some of the policy shifts that can enable more flexibility as well.

Mixed-Age Offerings

At the elementary level in particular, it is possible to add flexibility to the master schedule by combining multiple grade levels into one or more teams. For example, imagine a scenario with forty third-grade learners shared by two teachers and another forty fourth-grade learners shared by two other teachers. Rather than having two educator teams of two teachers at each grade level, there instead could be a single team of four educators sharing a mixed-age roster of eighty third and fourth graders. In this case, the operational complexity is reduced because rather than navigating two teams' schedules, you are now navigating only one. A shift to mixed-age rosters requires thoughtful support for educators and may be best employed in schools that are already making a shift to competency-based approaches. Mixed-aged, team-based models also allow more flexibility and innovation when schools are facing declining student enrollment.

Using Community Educators

Some schools that we've partnered with have created greater flexibility in their master schedules by partnering with local community-based organizations to provide high-interest electives during the same block of time during the day. This option is especially helpful when trying to create common planning time for educator teams who share larger, common rosters of students.

Take, for instance, the situation where one hundred students are shared by a team of four educators. To get common planning time, all those students must be somewhere else at the same time. That is a lot of students who will need options at once—a number that could quickly overwhelm most standard elective-based scheduling options. By bringing in multiple outside community-based organizations, it is possible to offer not only lots of programming simultaneously, but also a wider variety of options than what might be possible otherwise.

The context also shapes how community educators can be used. Some states require that community educators hold certain credentials or cannot be alone with groups of students without certified educators present. In most cases, there are creative solutions to these challenges that do not compromise the safety and learning of students.

For example, some schools have required their community educators to become certified substitutes and use those existing structures to vet and pay for these educators. In addition, the context helps to determine when students have access to these opportunities. In some schools, it may be daily for fifty minutes; in others, it might be once a week for ninety minutes. The schedule has to make sense for the students and the educator team, but also to the community educators. Coming in for fifty minutes one day a week may not be worth it to a community educator, but stacking together three fifty-minute classes on one day can create an interesting opportunity for someone like a paid teaching artist.

Virtual Electives

Similar to using community educators, virtual electives and other digital offerings can help build greater flexibility into team-based master schedules. Whether they are offered asynchronously, such as foreign language with Duolingo or artificial intelligence (AI)–based tutoring with Amira Learning, or synchronously, such as high-interest electives from ASU Prep Digital, virtual offerings create high levels of flexibility because there are fewer constraints with time and space. In fact, with synchronous offerings, there are actually advantages to having more students engaged in learning at the same time, such as allowing synchronous providers to meet minimum participant numbers to justify the cost of live instructors. These virtual synchronous options can also be provided locally. For example, a single Mandarin teacher could teach in person for two periods and then offer virtual class to the whole district for another three periods.

Seat-Time Flexibility

Recently passed legislation in Arizona has enabled school systems to change instructional models to accommodate flexible seat time. In flexible seat-time instructional models, "students still receive the required number of instructional hours, but such time can be satisfied through flexible and innovative solutions such as remote instruction, project-based learning, personalized and competency-based learning, or weekend and evening instruction."[4] Policies such as flexible seat time better enable innovations in both the delivery of instruction and when instruction happens, allowing master schedule configurations, such as Schedule Level 4, to be feasible and compliant. While there are shifts that can create master schedules without policies like flexible seat time, encouraging policy makers to consider this innovative approach to instructional time will better enable team-based staffing models to thrive.

CONSTRAINTS, UNINTENDED CONSEQUENCES, AND TRADE-OFFS

When implementing any new innovation in schools, there are always constraints, unintended consequences, and trade-offs that school leaders must accommodate. Master scheduling may be one of the activities in which these obstructions surface most saliently. For instance, many services for students with disabilities and services for multilingual learners statutorily require the tracking of instructional minutes. This may pose a challenge for scheduling, as there may be various points in the day at which educators must solely attend to students with disabilities or multilingual learners, or those learners must be taught in a different learning environment to meet their individualized education program (IEP) or language goals. A well-intentioned effort might be to group all students with disabilities or multilingual learners into one team, but from a bird's-eye view, these practices may actually be unintentionally exclusionary to those students. Regardless of the services that students receive, they should be placed in the least restrictive learning environment where all their needs are successfully met.

Class-size ratios can pose another constraint. If state legislation or school system working conditions promulgate a specific student-to-teacher ratio, this may pose a challenge to creating larger shared rosters of students. In some school systems, class-size ratios exist to ensure that educators have a prep period. While a challenge, school leaders implementing team-based staffing models have made trade-offs for larger student-to-teacher ratios. For instance, in exchange for taking on more students on a shared roster, school leaders are able to flex time differently to provide more time for protected, collaborative planning time. Adam Unrien, the principal of Smith Junior High School, proposed this to his teachers. He offered that they could have four classes with thirty-seven students each instead of five classes with thirty students. This created two shared planning periods for the educator team. Although the team was initially hesitant, they discussed it and decided on the additional shared planning time. Asking for input from your educator teams about when they would like their planning time may actually uncover opportunities for flexibility. Some educator teams may prefer a singular large block of time to collaborate, while others may rather have two smaller blocks of time at different points of the day.

Another consideration for team-based models is recognizing that teaming doesn't happen all day long. The underlying structure of teams makes scheduling more flexible, but at certain parts of the day, classrooms may resemble one educator instructing a single group of students. It is important to consider which educators are instructionally and pedagogically capable of managing a larger group of students. Perhaps more seasoned educators take on larger groups of students, while more novice educators take on smaller groups. While this may ultimately be a decision that is left up to the team, the range of experience and abilities is a worthwhile consideration when forming your first team.

Finally, ensuring that students still have access to singular course offerings is pertinent. Courses in the performing arts, visual arts, world languages, physical education, and other advanced subject areas are still critical. Electives may assist you in forming your teams and may even add an element of depth to your teams. One way to do this is to create shared elective blocks that allow students from multiple teams to participate in specialized courses. Another way to make schedules work for students who want to be in courses like band or Advanced Placement (AP) Spanish is to place them on the same team.

CONCLUDING THOUGHTS ON THE MASTER SCHEDULE

Central to the work of building team-based staffing models is the master schedule. The master schedule is the key mechanism that can enable—or hinder—innovative teaching and learning conditions. If we could summarize this chapter into a phrase, it would be that as you build your master schedule for teams, you should ensure that that *the same educators have the same students at the same time.* Educator teams must have the autonomy to use their time as they see fit (within established policy parameters, of course) so they are able to dynamically group and regroup students to better meet their needs. Simultaneously, you must build the schedule in a way that enables educator teams to have a common planning time. In chapter 6, we will detail the different ways to consider creating shared, flexible learning environments that better enable team-based educators to use their newly constructed schedule in the most effective ways.

CHAPTER 6

Creating Shared, Flexible Learning Environments

For decades, scientists have conducted experiments in isolated, compartmentalized labs. Their workspaces are separated by walls, floors, and even entire buildings. These design parameters provide private, controlled environments, unintentionally decreasing the opportunities for scientists to collaborate.

Sometimes private, controlled environments are necessary. However, there is a long history of how some of the most important breakthroughs in science came through collaboration and the exchange of ideas, even across very different areas of study. The physical environment plays a role in encouraging collaboration. A 2014 study found that scientists who crossed paths more frequently—in stairwells, the hallway, or common areas—were more likely to talk with one another and engage in collaborative projects.[1] On the other hand, scientists who had more physical distance were less likely to work together. The major lesson was that small changes that increased proximity significantly influenced the opportunities for, and dynamics of, collaboration.

The example of the perambulating scientists holds a few key lessons for anyone thinking about implementing team-based staffing models. First, physical proximity of educators to one another, especially those on teams, is important. Second, the design of the physical space can affect outcomes that might not be obvious at first blush. Third, you do not need to totally reconstruct spaces to implement strategic school staffing.

We open this chapter with key considerations as you construct learning environments for educator teams. Knowing that leaders will be working with a wide range of existing buildings, we then offer a framework for thinking about spaces. This Continuum of Learning Environments serves as a tool to consider what is currently available on your campus and to support decision-making for transforming learning spaces over time. We conclude the chapter by offering suggestions of new learning zones that other teams have designed and a concrete process for creating new learning environments.

KEY CONSIDERATIONS FOR TEAM-BASED LEARNING SPACES

One of the most common questions we receive in our work is, "Do I need to construct an entirely new school building to have effective team-based models?" Fortunately, the answer to this question is a resounding *no*. Schools don't need to tear down walls or pass a facilities bond to enable teaming. Learning spaces matter, *and* there are ways to think about reimagining space that are feasible in the most traditional school buildings and with limited budgets.

As you identify the shared learning environment of your first educator team, we offer three key considerations to keep in mind, which will be discussed next:

- Prioritize proximity
- Design for flexibility
- Support new uses of space

Prioritize Proximity

The most essential and first consideration as you identify the educator team's physical space is ensuring close proximity for educators. For some, this may mean moving educators into different classrooms on campus. For others, this may mean moving teams into existing pods with moveable walls.

When Principal Adam Unrien launched teams at Smith Junior High School, he quickly recognized the limitations imposed by the proximity of the school's educators. Teachers were isolated in subject-specific areas of the school. "What we did with teaming was put the educators on teams next to each other so that they had the freedom to move kids around based on areas of expertise and the trusted adult they connected with," he said. "By bringing those teachers together, it allowed for more dynamic use of space and greater flexibility in how we engaged students." His simple reorganization of teachers next door to one another enabled them to work closely together.

Whatever your situation, putting educators as close to each other as possible unlocks the potential of team-based models in two key areas: collaboration and dynamic student grouping.

Collaboration. Just like our scientists, when educators are in close proximity to each other, the opportunities to learn together and support each other increase greatly. Even in the most traditional spaces, educators who are located in adjacent classrooms check in with each other more often. They give updates to each other about students in quick hallway conversations, and they are able to provide support to each other at the exact moment that it is needed.

Dynamic student grouping. In addition to a master schedule that ensures the educator team has the *same students* at the *same time*, close proximity of the educator team makes dynamic student grouping (and regrouping) possible. Educator teams may post schedules for the day on the door when students arrive at the beginning of the day or the class period. Alternatively, educators may introduce a lesson to the entire group of students and then break them out into smaller groups based on student choice or need. Close physical proximity minimizes transition time and also allows quick adjustments in real time.

Design for Flexibility

"Schools are designed for teachers. They should be designed for learning," states Krista Adams, former principal of Stevenson Elementary. Flexibility in learning spaces supports the variations among learners and the ways that they learn best.

All spaces can be used for learning. Start by considering *all* spaces in a school building as learning spaces. It's likely that you have access to large amounts of space in your building beyond the current classroom walls that could be repurposed for learning in team-based contexts. These include:

- Outdoor spaces
- Hallways and atria
- Libraries
- Art studios
- Gymnasiums and cafeterias
- Auditoriums
- Unused offices and closets

- Outdated lab spaces
- Football stadiums and athletic facilities

Repurposing spaces may include modifying the function of existing spaces. For example, an existing library furnished primarily with bookshelves can be converted to a learning commons with interactive meeting spaces, access to print and digital resources, and quiet research pods that can be reserved by an educator team. Repurposing spaces may also include creating dual-purposed spaces. For instance, hallways may also be used as one-on-one conference areas or group presentation spaces.

When educator teams begin to view the entire campus as a learning space, many new opportunities will present themselves. At Westwood High School, a large hallway nook with large floor-to-ceiling glass windows and high seating at counters became a small group learning space with the addition of tables and chairs. It's now one of the most in-demand spaces for educator teams.

Design for varied modalities and configurations. Team-based staffing models help educators deliver on the promise of deeper and personalized learning for all students. To be truly student-centered, physical environments should support different types of learning activities and student learning styles. When an educator team supports a shared roster of students, many more adult-to-student configurations become possible. The learning environment should be designed to maximize the potential of these configurations. School leaders and educator teams may want to design for the following:

- **Community gathering:** Teams may want to meet as a whole group for morning assembly and need a space that will accommodate a larger group of students comfortably. Educator teams often use this time for community building and setting shared expectations. The community space can also be used for guest expert presentations or student showcases.
- **Varied group sizes:** Teams may want to break into different-sized groups for instruction based on myriad factors, including subject area, student interest, and level of support needed. One week, a team may decide to utilize groups of 15:1 for math instruction and 4:1 for reading instruction, and they will need flexible ways to accommodate those different plans.

- **Varied learning modalities:** Teams may adapt learning environments based on learning type throughout the day. For example, consider what space might look like for students giving and receiving feedback on one another's work versus creating a new solution to combat climate change.

Regardless of team composition, being able to flex and move throughout the day in response to learner needs is a hallmark of effective shared space. As you map your learning space design, return to your *why* for launching team-based models. If your school is focused on science, technology, engineering, arts, and mathematics (STEAM) instruction, your design should reflect this priority. Work in collaboration with educators (and students!) to envision the experience of learners, and then design the physical space from there.

Design with safety and policy in mind. Creating more flexible learning spaces can and should be done with consideration for maintaining safety. As you reimagine your space, consider the lines of sight for all educators in the room or group of classrooms. At least one educator should have a line of sight to any given student at all times. Consider how many lines of sight each space has and where educators are likely to be positioned in the learning space throughout the day.

Creating flexible learning environments with intentional lines of sight offers the benefit of providing more autonomy for learners. If multiple educators are able to monitor multiple sections of the learning space, learners will be able to move more flexibly and independently to support their learning goals. In more traditional classroom spaces, educators can open their classroom doors to create lines of sight, especially during transition times.

Ample lines of sight also create the ability to oversee noncertified team members. If your local context demands that noncertified educators or community members be accompanied by a certified educator when in the presence of students, multiple lines of sight can allow educator teams to better use extended team members such as student teachers, tutors, volunteers, and other community educators.

Support New Uses of Space

Given our longstanding tradition of assigning teachers to classrooms in schools across the United States, both educators and students will need support in thinking differently about how space is used throughout the building and by a team throughout a school day. Just because a team has newfound access to a hallway, rearranged furniture, or a new glass door between classrooms doesn't mean that educators and learners will start using their space differently. For educators, supporting this change will require setting aside time for teams to plan how they will reimagine and use their new space. For students, supporting this change will require creating new systems and structures for how they move through the learning space. Greg Mendez of Skyline High School advises, "Early teams need to think about their mindsets around teaming and the use of space. I wish I would have done this." Here are a few considerations to keep in mind.

Supporting shifts for educators. One of the most memorable moments in the journey to becoming a teacher is the first time that we each get our "own" classrooms. Even for those who are excited about launching team-based models, the shift away from this tradition can be unsettling. It's worth taking the time to talk explicitly about this change and what it means for educators and students alike.

To make possible the shifts that we have described previously, educator teams will need time to reenvision how space will be used. In collaboration with school leaders, the team may want to step back and consider the combined learning space as a whole and how it can be designed for flexible modalities and configurations. As Principal Mendez says, "Sharing space is about getting away from the 'This is my classroom, you can't have a key' mindset. Spaces that are designed for specific learning can help with this; for example, a room for direct instruction, a room for collaboration, a room for labs, a room for small groups, etc."

For instance, if an elementary educator team has access to three traditional classrooms, perhaps one classroom becomes the community gathering space, with a few independent workstations at the edge of the room; another classroom holds enough desks or student workstations to accommodate more traditional, whole-group instruction and has whiteboards on the walls; the third classroom includes a classroom library and reading area and ample seating for small-group instruction. The educator team shares all these spaces across the shared instructional time.

Questions will arise for educators, and these should be viewed as opportunities for conversation and alignment. Some educators will wonder about where to put their stuff, while others will wonder whether they still get to decorate the learning environment. Some may ask what happens to the teachers' desks and whether they'll have a classroom that is just for them. In many team-based models, teacher desks do exist, and teachers get to decorate the shared learning space. Our recommendation is that you keep returning to the learning experiences that you want students to have and make decisions together, with that vision as your guide.

Supporting shifts for students. Educator teams that strategically share spaces create new opportunities to establish student-centered learning and belonging. At Westwood High School, educator teams label their doors with their team name—for example, "Academy of Curious Minds." At Stevenson Elementary, the kindergarten team labels each classroom with a "kinder-garden" name: "Water," "Cactus," "Bee," or "Bloom." The signal to students is "This is *our* space" rather than "This is *my* space."

Creating shared flexible learning spaces, however, also demands clear communication and support so learners know when and how to move through learning spaces. Are learners self-directed, or do they move based on instruction from the team? How often will learning spaces flex, and how will students learn how to move through those new spaces when changes are made? Students will need support during this transition to shared space, and school leaders can work with educator teams to identify the scaffolds that need to be put into place for learners.

In the Stevenson Elementary "kinder-garden" led by lead teacher Taylor Murphy, the educator team uses images to represent each room (e.g., a cactus, a flower) when displaying student names for dynamic student groupings. They have placed footprints on the floor to show students the walking path for transitions. During the first month of the school year, teachers rotated through the learning environments and students stayed in one room, and over several months, the team worked to build dynamic student groupings, with students moving between spaces.

With older students, educator teams might consider implementing a system like Levels of Student Autonomy (see our Authors' Page for a resource link). The autonomy levels provide shared language for how, where, when, and with whom students can work. Students move up to the next level and gain independence as they demonstrate success at handling increased choice. With scaffolds in place, shared space can help learners develop agency. A student who needs to ask another teacher a clarifying question about an assignment—an interdisciplinary project, for example—can get assistance immediately by going to a nearby classroom. The student can advocate to get the necessary help from the adult who can best provide that support—a benefit that emerges from an educator team with shared space.

CONTINUUM OF LEARNING ENVIRONMENTS

We find it helpful to think about flexible learning spaces along a continuum with investments in enhancements that can happen over time. Many schools start the work of team-based staffing with only modest changes to furniture and resources. Often, this is as simple as putting educators on a team in classrooms next to one another.

You don't need to build a brand new school building to start teaming, *and* there are changes that you and your teams will want to make in terms of how you reimagine existing space and consider new spaces you may need. When launching your first team, you may start on the lower end of the continuum by making nominal changes to physical space and taking on larger-scale changes as teaming spreads across more of your campus.

As shown in table 6.1, the continuum includes four general levels of investment in space. Level 1 represents changes you can make with little to no new capital investment. Level 4 represents completely redesigned learning spaces. We should expect some fuzziness between the levels. In fact, we should be less concerned about whether a space is a particular level and instead use the continuum as a framework to support decision-making for a phased approach for transforming learning spaces. Importantly, the continuum underscores the mindset that you don't need expensively redesigned spaces for team-based staffing models to flourish.

Level 1

Level 1 is the simplest to achieve: it includes putting educators on a team in close proximity to one another in preexisting classrooms. The full team may meet as one large group in a classroom, the hallway, or another nearby space in the morning to preview plans for the day, and again at the end of the day to close out their time together. Otherwise, students and educators will be moving through existing classroom spaces throughout the day. Educators may flex learning spaces within existing classrooms, primarily through the use of existing furniture.

TABLE 6.1 Different levels and their associated physical spaces and resource changes

	Level 1	*Level 2*	*Level 3*	*Level 4*
Level description	Use existing spaces that are physically close to one another.	Invest in lower-cost furniture, equipment, and/or minor construction.	Invest in higher-cost furniture, equipment, and/or major construction.	Invest in completely redesigned space or new construction.
Physical spaces	• Identify adjacent classrooms that can be allocated to a team. • Identify and outfit a space (if possible) where the whole team can be together even for short periods (e.g., cafeteria, library, auditorium, open classrooms, outside areas when possible). • Identify school spaces beyond the immediate classroom vicinity that may be repurposed for team-based learning. • Change one-teacher, one-classroom visual cues (e.g., individual teachers' names on classrooms) to cues that reinforce the team-based approach (e.g., all teachers' names on all classrooms or abandoning teachers' names altogether and instead naming classrooms after content or culturally relevant connections—authors, biomes, local landmarks). • Ensure that students' names, learning processes, and work are displayed across the entire learning space.	• Add cut-throughs or glass windows/doors between classroom spaces to allow more movement among existing space and improved lines of sight. • Add garage-style doors between spaces that can be opened and closed on demand.	• Knock down walls to create a more open and flexible learning space with particular zones or areas to support different learning configurations (whole team, small groups, individual work). • New construction of shared learning spaces outside team-based classrooms (e.g., reconfigured libraries, cafeterias, or highly flexible spaces like "black box theaters," a simple performance space with black walls).	
Furniture and resources	• Arrange or modify existing furniture in new ways to meet learning needs (e.g., take the legs off some student desks to create high and low working spaces).	• Replace existing furniture with tables and chairs at different heights and sizes, signaling different learning experiences. • Augment existing learning materials that allow more collaborative student work products (e.g., presentation sharing from personal devices, vertical whiteboards).	• Replace existing student desks and furniture with flexible, modular furniture of different shapes and sizes to include couches, chairs, and other pieces that better approximate real-world working environments.	

The Power of Proximity

We met with our team leads and handed them some research on the power of proximity for learning. We then grabbed the school map and worked with them to carve out space and classrooms that they were comfortable with.

—Greg Mendez, principal, Skyline High School

One of the ways in which I have seen our educators create flexible space is through their flexible seating and table arrangements. We had several classrooms where they varied the height of their tables to allow for different learning experiences. A specific example was in my counseling classroom. I had a table that was low to the ground to allow for students to sit on pillows or crisscross. I had standing tables toward the back. Then I had more traditional tables with the option for traditional seating or workout balls. These same ideas were highlighted in multiple classrooms on our campus. The most interesting space that I saw this past year was in kindergarten. The teacher had used a bunk bed for their reading space. Students could read and hang out under the bed in a small library space, or could climb to the top and sit alongside peers.

—Ally Gilardi, counselor, Hermosa Vista Elementary School

Level 2

Level 2 includes investments in lower-cost furniture and/or minor construction to create more shared, inclusive, and flexible space. For example, a team may work across the same four adjacent classrooms but add double glass doors between classrooms to improve traffic flow and lines of sight between spaces. The team may also augment existing furniture with new resources that support teaming, such as swapping tables for individual student desks and purchasing vertical whiteboards on wheels.

Changing Mindsets About Space

When we can't change the building, we have to change our mindset. We fit one hundred sixth graders on the floor of a classroom for ten-to-fifteen-minute mini-lessons before dividing into other learning spaces for work time. Our campus was built in the 1980s with semipermanent divider walls that we were able to take down and move. We also utilize extended staff members. Intervention groups were often led by specials teachers in their own respective spaces during times when they were not actively teaching. Our library is also quite large and allows for many groups of students to be simultaneously using the learning space.

—Shay Quitno, sixth-grade lead teacher, Hermosa Vista Elementary School

Level 3

Level 3 learning environments often signal a larger, schoolwide commitment to team-based staffing and typically come about when teaming is expanding and deepening throughout a school. Traditional classroom walls may be torn down and replaced with larger, open spaces that allow high levels of flexibility and movement. Flexible learning zones comprise the entire learning environment, and there is often no discernible space that belongs to one educator or set of students.

Level 4

Finally, level 4 is the least common example on the continuum, as it requires the greatest amount of time and financial commitment for a school and school system—though, we also know that these spaces do exist in some places! We know that a level 4 learning environment is not needed to implement effective team-based staffing models. It's also exciting to think about how school buildings of the future could be designed in fundamentally new and better ways. Just as most people working in the knowledge economy no longer work in isolated, one-person offices behind closed doors all day, so could there be a future in which teachers and students aren't isolated in small rooms with rows of desks.

Should you be in the position to design a new building, we encourage you not to build a rectangle with a bunch of squares inside it. You and your larger school community have the opportunity to create a space that does not reinforce the traditional grammar of schooling, and instead to create intentional learning spaces that allow teams of educators to meet students' needs dynamically and flexibly. For inspiration, we recommend Robert Dillon and Rebecca Hare's book *The Space: A Guide for Leaders.*[2] Or maybe plan a visit to Ehrman Crest Elementary and Middle Schools in western Pennsylvania, where their school design earned a place among *Time* magazine's two hundred best inventions of 2022.[3]

NEW LEARNING ZONES

Once you have a rough sense of where on the continuum your first teams will be working, the next step is to begin to consider how you will use the area *within* your existing learning spaces. Team-based, student-centered learning environments often benefit from creating multiple learning zones.

As we shared throughout this chapter, your space should support the learning needs of your students. Although you may believe that they would benefit from all these learning zones, realistically, you might need to focus in the beginning on designing one or two that you believe will have the greatest impact. We have seen educator teams start with one learning space design and continue to modify, adjust, and add as they, and their students, become more comfortable working in new ways.

PROCESS FOR CREATING NEW LEARNING ENVIRONMENTS

Like all aspects of planning to launch team-based staffing models, creating new learning environments should not happen in isolation, but rather with a diverse group of key actors who bring multiple strengths and perspectives. Most importantly, the students and educators who will be using these new spaces should have significant input on their creation. You may want to consider the following action steps as you begin the process of creating your own shared flexible learning spaces that support team-based staffing models.

Start with Values and Outcomes

Link back to your *why for teaming*. What do you plan to achieve via team-based models, and how can your learning spaces reflect those outcomes? Consider where you want to begin on the continuum in your launch year and what is feasible given your time, capacity, and budget. Start small. Experiment and consider which changes might have disproportionately large impacts on student and educator outcomes in future years.

Solicit Student and Community Input

Ask students, as the primary users of any classroom, what they want from their learning spaces. Consider asking questions like the following:

- What types of spaces help you learn?
- What types of spaces make you feel most welcome? Most comfortable?
- Where do you feel the most engaged in your learning at school? How about outside school?
- What are a few things that you wish you could change about your learning space?
- What learning spaces do you want to make sure our school keeps?

Soliciting input from community members can also help identify which aspects of the school building adults feel connected to and how well the school building is meeting people's needs. Ask educators, staff, guardians, local architects, and community educators what they want from school spaces using questions like the following:

- Which spaces in the school help you feel the most connected to the vision of the school? To students? To other educators?
- What is currently working about your learning space? What could be improved?
- What changes would you make to learning environments to promote deeper and more personalized learning? To increase student engagement? How about student agency?

As you solicit input, keep in mind that almost everyone knows, and has direct experience with, the one-teacher, one-classroom paradigm of staffing schools. Listen for responses that might be reinforcing a teacher-centered approach and ask follow-up questions to better understand what community members value most.

Walk Your School and Document What You See

One of the easiest ways to identify what is possible is to walk around your entire school site and audit its current state against your intended values and outcomes. As you explore your campus, document your answers to the following questions:

- How welcoming are your entryways? Office spaces? Classroom spaces?
- Are your spaces equally welcoming for all members of your school community (e.g., all students, educators, support staff, specialists, families, community members)?
- Why are particular educators assigned to particular spaces? Are there any circumstances in which it would be politically difficult to move an educator (e.g., the person has accumulated thirty-five years of stuff in the classroom) or pedagogically unsound (e.g., the chemistry teacher needs daily access to sinks and the fume hood)?
- What are your unused or underutilized spaces?
- What spaces could be easily converted to shared space?
- What spaces could you repurpose?

Ideate and Visualize What Is Possible

To visualize what is possible, take the values and outcomes you identified, the input you received, and the audit you conducted and translate them into ideas. Break out the whiteboards, create an idea wall, design a storyboard, or draw new learning space layouts. What changes could you make that align your *why for teaming* and your vision for learning spaces? It may be helpful to group the changes that you want to make into small, medium, and large changes. What improvements can you make in a matter of days versus the reconfigurations that may take weeks, months, or even years?

CONCLUDUING THOUGHTS ON LEARNING SPACES

Space is one of the most visible aspects of the traditional one-teacher, one-classroom model, and it is not only a challenging mental model to break out of, but can be a costly one to redo. Even if school learning environments were totally redesigned and rebuilt to accommodate team-based staffing, educators could still default to teaching their single roster of students all day in the corner of a room. It is the educator team's mindset about space that will be essential to creating shared, flexible learning environments. You don't need to turn your school into a construction zone to build educator teams—space is all about how it is seen and used.

In chapter 7, we will describe the pervasive systems that uphold the one-teacher, one-classroom model. Although they are not as physically visible as the walls that often reinforce our ideas of traditional staffing, they reinforce all the invisible aspects of the grammar of schooling. Working within and/or redesigning these systems will be another key aspect of enabling your team-based staffing models.

CHAPTER 7

Team-Based Staffing in a World of One-Teacher, One-Classroom Systems and Structures

When surveying potential electric vehicle (EV) buyers about what was holding them back from purchasing an EV, researchers from the University of Texas at Arlington found the results given in table 7.1.[1]

Given the relatively small number of EVs in the automobile market in 2023, the cost of purchasing such a vehicle and replacement batteries make sense as barriers. As the total number of EVs continues to increase and as the technology improves, we'll naturally expect prices to fall. But the other three barriers are related to challenges of having an EV in a world built for gas-powered cars.

Any time an innovation involves a paradigm shift from the way that things are typically done, there naturally are challenges and inconveniences because, simply put, most systems and structures were not created for the new paradigm. For example, in 2024, there were more than 145,000 gas stations in the United States compared to 61,000 charging stations—and that number was only 29,000 in 2020. Despite a burgeoning EV market and concrete investments in building EV infrastructure, most systems and structures still reinforce, and are reinforced by, gas-powered cars. As the percentage of EVs sold continues to increase, the supporting infrastructure will continue to grow.

Much like the paradigm shift from gas to electric cars, the shift to team-based staffing models requires changes to the infrastructure that undergirds schooling. From communicating with families to professional learning for

TABLE 7.1 Top reasons provided as barriers to purchasing an electric vehicle

Barrier	*Mean*	*Rank*	*Paradigm shift–related?*
High purchase price	4.29	1	No
Insufficient number of public charging stations	4.16	2	Yes
High battery replacement cost	4.12	3	No
Insufficient maintenance and repair services	3.99	4	Yes
Adaptation cost of electrical system at home	3.93	5	Yes

educators to simply taking attendance, there are a range of systems and structures that make a school function. Most school-level systems start from the assumption that an individual teacher works with a single group of students in a specific place during a set period of time—the one-teacher, one-classroom model. Although erecting team-based staffing models within these existing systems is possible, better-aligned school-level system solutions become necessary over time. Take the advice of Jan Vesley, former superintendent of Kyrene School District: "Spend a significant amount of time early on thinking through some of the barriers that you may face with teams and then develop solutions to those barriers."

In this chapter, we highlight some of the most frequently identified school-level systems and structures that need to be reexamined when moving to team-based staffing. We also offer short-term solutions to address these compatibility issues. While we try to focus on the school level, some of these systems and structures are actually implemented at the level of the educator teams. We have included team-level systems and structures here because we have seen advantages to taking a whole-school approach to navigating these changes—in so doing, school leaders increase the likelihood that teams can learn from each other. In addition, students and families experience greater coherence as they move from one team to the next over the course of their time in school.

What we are intentionally not discussing in this chapter is infrastructure that exists at the school-system level, including potential challenges like collective bargaining agreements, curricular adoptions, and site-level control of budgets. We believe that those things are critically important, but given the audience of this book, they go beyond the scope of this discussion.

WHICH SYSTEMS AND STRUCTURES ARE CHALLENGING?

When asked to identify which school-level systems and structures were particularly challenging to building-level leaders implementing team-based staffing models, their responses generally fall into three broad categories:

- Systems associated with students and families
- Systems associated with educators
- Systems associated with school operations

There are clearly challenges that cut across multiple categories. For example, knowing where students are physically located at any given time is a challenge in both the "students and families" category and the "school operations" category. The particular categorization is less important than considering whether this structure or system might be a challenge in your context, and if so, how you might address it. Although there are dozens of possible challenges, for each category we selected three of those most frequently cited by school leaders implementing their first team-based models. We list these challenges, by category, in table 7.2 and further describe them in the sections that follow.

Systems Associated with Students and Families

Family communication and engagement. One of the biggest challenges when moving to team-based staffing models relates to communication. Often, we think about this challenge related to how educators are communicating with one another, but a similar challenge relates to how the educator team communicates with students' families and vice versa. There is power in being a unified front and efficiencies in distributing the responsibility of family communication and engagement.

TABLE 7.2 Selection of systems and structures that school leaders identify frequently as challenging when implementing team-based staffing models

Students and families	*Educators*	*School operations*
Family communication Family-based events at school Students and families recognizing and appreciating educators	Coaching and professional learning Coordinating the extended team (paraeducators, community educators) Planning time	Taking attendance and locating students Tracking instructional minutes Accessing data

The first aspect of challenges around family communication is how two-way communication works when it is not simply one teacher in one classroom. We have seen many teams, serving all ages of learners, tackle the outbound communication by leaning into specific roles and particular relationships. For example, some teams identify a designated educator who is responsible for soliciting input from the broader team and then producing a family newsletter or team email on an agreed-upon timeline.

It is also important for families to have a clear way of communicating with the team. Should families reach out to a single point of contact on the team? Should the team create a shared email account to which all communication can be directed? Should the team subdivide the roster into "advisories," where each educator on a team has a particular clutch of students for whom the person is specifically responsible and to whom any communication should be directed? We've seen schools implement all these strategies successfully. At this point, we don't have any empirical data to suggest one approach over the other, but we do feel strongly that it is essential that every educator team has a clear and easy answer to the question from families, "Who should I contact if I have a question or concern?"

Once family communication channels are established, it is important that there are systems and structures to ensure that the team is keeping track of communications with families, responding promptly, and ensuring that every teammate has access to those conversations. In business and industry, a team working with a shared group of clients would likely employ SalesForce or similar customer relationship management (CRM) software. These tools are specifically designed to strengthen and unify communication among the team members and between the team and the client.

In education, especially in traditional staffing models, the need for a CRM is not obvious. Individual educators often have personal systems for keeping track of family communications, but only rarely do other educators need access to that information. This is not true when working on a team, and it is imperative to have a way for educators sharing the common roster of students to have access to the whole team's communication with families. Some student information systems or student/family engagement systems (e.g., ClassDojo) have ways to add multiple educators who share a class of students, but this almost always involves changing some default settings or using clever workarounds.

With greater shared access to communications, educator teams can be more intentional about how they are working with families. They may identify a particular teammate to set up and manage the system and lead a portion of shared planning time related to family communication to which they bring insights ("As a team, we have not reached out to DeAndre's family in several weeks") and questions ("We agreed to make a positive phone call home to Mellisa; who is going to do that?").

To address challenges around family communication and engagement, we have seen schools implementing team-based staffing models adopt strategies like a shared family communication log. Whether it is through an existing communication and logging system that accommodates multiple educators sharing a common roster of learners or through a solution created and customized by the team, it is imperative that each team have a way of keeping track of, and making transparent, family communications. For an example, please see the Authors' Page.

Family-based events at school. There are many high-profile moments when families and schools come together. Perhaps two of the most visible are "Meet the Teacher Night" and parent-teacher conferences—which, as their names suggest, are deeply rooted in the one-teacher, one-classroom approach to staffing schools. Team-based staffing models provide the perfect opportunity to refresh the purpose and form factor of both of these events.

From the first week of each new school year, a "Meet the Team Night" makes it clear that each student will have a team of adults supporting him or her. The simple rebranding from "teacher" to "team" represents a significant opportunity to begin to shift families' mindsets around the traditional grammar of school. This should not be the first time that families are learning about a shift to team-based staffing, but it is a chance for teams to broadcast their distributed expertise and how, together, they will be better able to meet each learner's varied needs. A sample agenda for a one-hour "Meet the Team" night might look something like this for a four-educator team:

- Whole-group—everyone in the same physical space (5 min)
    - Power of a team-based approach
    - Meet the team and our superpowers

- Small-group rotations—divide group into quarters and rotate (10 min each)
    - "Who do I call?": How family communication will work this year
    - "What are we learning this year?": High-level overview of key projects, books, and learning outcomes
    - "Does teamwork make the dream work?": Game/experience in which families experience the power of teams firsthand
    - "What advice do you have?": Family panel from the previous year
- Half-groups—bring two groups together with two educators (15 min)
    - Ask us anything
    - Question-and-answer period

On a logistical level, it is sometimes necessary to divide the students alphabetically and run through the agenda a couple of times on one day or across two days to ensure that there is ample room for all students and families who plan to attend.

A second compatibility issue with team-based staffing models arises during what are traditionally known as "parent-teacher conferences." Many of the school leaders with whom we work with have rebranded these "family-team conferences." Teams take many different approaches to how to divide up the conferences:

- **Entire team with every family:** Given the sheer number of conversations, conferences done with the whole team can almost never be done during standard conferencing windows. Instead, they are strategically spread out over the course of several weeks or even months. The goal ends up being something like, "Meet with every family at least twice this year, and others more frequently as needed."
- **Some fraction of the team with some fraction of the families:** Educators on the core team may partner together and/or include educators on the extended team to meet with a subset of the families.
- **Single educators with a strategic subset of families:** Ultimately, this option ends up looking and feeling the most familiar. What sets these conferences apart is the inclusion of perspectives from other team members, either in writing or in video recordings.

Regardless of what strategy the team adopts, in the days and weeks leading up to conferences, the whole team is using collaborative planning time to norm (agree upon expectations, language, and key messaging) and decide what are the most salient points for each conversation. In addition, by involving all the team members, it can be possible to offer a great diversity of time slots to families. For example, some teams may schedule a portion of their collaborative planning blocks for virtual conferences, something that has become ever more practical given the ubiquity of video-based meetings postpandemic.

Finally, in step with larger trends, some schools have entirely abandoned the idea of team-family conferences in favor of experiences that are more student-centered (e.g., student-led conferences). In these cases, students lead their families through demonstrations of their learning, which can range from formal presentations to simply showing a set of work products. Many team-based models create the conditions for the deep, cross-disciplinary projects that bring about exceptional student-led conferences.

To address challenges associated with team-based staffing and family-focused events often oriented around single-teacher models, partner schools have adopted at least one of the following strategies:

- **Rebrand your events:** One of the easiest things that you can do to better align family-centered events with team-based staffing is simply to change the names. As already indicated, "Meet the Teacher Night" becomes "Meet the Team Night." "Parent-teacher conference" becomes "parent-team conference." Clearly, the content and format must also change, but don't underestimate the power that rebranding can have on your school's larger culture around teaming.
- **Create new, team-centered events:** As you launch your first team, consider whether there are new events that you want to try that might feel more doable now with educator teams. For example, we have school partners that have created quarterly "curriculum nights," when families can come and get a sense of what students will be working on for the next nine weeks across various content areas.

Students and families recognizing and appreciating educators. A final and somewhat surprising challenge in family engagement is related to recognizing and appreciating educators. This challenge is especially acute in the elementary context. In the one-teacher, one-classroom staffing model, it is clear whom you are recognizing, and in many cases that is a single individual (although that point should probably be more deeply considered). If you used to buy a holiday present or give a gift card for coffee during Teacher Appreciation Week, do you (indeed, can you) still do that when your child has five educators, not just one? Schools that have been implementing team-based staffing models have started to centralize the recognition and celebrations of educators, which has gone a long way to ensure that all members of the educator teams are recognized and families are able to fully participate without breaking the bank, given how many educators may be supporting their child.

To address challenges associated with families recognizing and appreciating educators, several of our partner schools have adopted at least one of the following strategies:

- **School-level coordination around educator appreciation:** Some schools create a schedule for the week that allows a mix of individual and educator-team recognition.

Teacher Appreciation Week Schedule at Altura Preparatory School

Monday, May 6: Class Bouquets! We ask each student to bring three to four flowers (garden-picked, store-bought, or handmade) to add to their teachers' vases to make a beautiful, unique bouquet for their teachers to enjoy all week long. Do you have a green thumb or are skilled in making floral arrangements? Sign up **[HERE]** to help make and deliver floral arrangements for the teachers and staff. Don't forget to bring your floral stem cutters and clippers!

Tuesday, May 7: Special Treats! Remember your teachers and bring them each a special treat. Click **[HERE]** for a list of your teachers' favorite treats.

Wednesday, May 8: Noteworthy Gifts! Please have your child write each of their teachers a special note or a handwritten card to let them know how much they have affected their life this year or what makes that teacher so very special.

Thursday, May 9: Teacher Swag Day! Bring a special gift of your choice for your teachers. Click **[HERE]** for a list of some of your teachers' favorite things.

Friday, May 10: Color Their World! Have your child draw, paint, or color a special picture for at least one of the teachers on their team, thanking them for an incredible year!

- **Team-based recognition from students/student councils:** At some schools, and secondary schools in particular, recognition of teachers may fall more to students than families. In those cases, the same basic logic applies: How do we take an established practice and reorient it to help reinforce team-based staffing models? For example, during Teacher Appreciation Week, members of the student council may decorate each teacher's door. This can still be done, but maybe rather than individual teachers, the recognition is for the team; and rather than decorating just the doors, a section of the hallway shared by each team can be decorated. Rather than hosting a lunch for all faculty together, students could bring food, snacks, or coffee to teachers during their collaborative planning meeting.
- **Teacher versus educator versus team appreciation:** As a community, we should work to acknowledge that it takes a team, even in nonteam-based staffing models, to successfully educate young learners. We should continue to appropriately celebrate professional teachers, and it is helpful to think about appreciation and recognition more broadly. This will go a long way toward helping to build appreciation for the myriad roles that all sorts of educators play in a team-based staffing model. Perhaps during "Educator Team Appreciation Week," there are specific days that call out the contributions of specific types of educators (community educators, paraeducators, preservice educators, professional educators, educational leaders) and recognize all of them as essential workers in improving outcomes for all.

Systems Associated with Educators

Professional learning and educator coaching. Based on current research, the United States spends more than $18 billion on professional learning for educators each year.[2] The vast majority of that professional learning is based on the one-teacher, one-classroom model of staffing schools, and many approaches are designed so every educator at a school site receives the same content at the same time. A transition to team-based staffing models provides school leadership with a unique opportunity to rethink professional learning and coaching for the whole school.

Many sites still offer whole-school professional learning. Whether that is in the week before school starts or during built-in professional learning days throughout the year, it is not uncommon to see the whole faculty learning about a particular topic together. Even in the best implementations of this model, such an approach misses two profound opportunities afforded by a team-based staffing model. First, with teaming, it is likely that not every educator needs to be equally skilled at all aspects of the job. This begs the question: Does the whole faculty *really* need to participate? Or could it be a representative from each team who is becoming the go-to expert? Second, given that educators (like our young learners) are invariably at different levels of understanding on any topic, is any whole-school professional learning appropriately differentiated? Given the roster of learners, the educators who serve them, and the curricular ambitions, is this topic even the most relevant? There will always be content in which every educator needs a common level of knowledge, skill, and mindset; however, we believe that that is more often the exception than the rule.

With respect to the power of professional learning, there are even stronger outcomes associated with educator coaching.[3] For that reason, we are especially interested in continuing to study the implications of team-based staffing models for coaching educators. First, and most obviously, it is possible for a coach to work with small groups of educators on the same team at the same time. For example, rather than having twenty-four individual conversations about the implementation of a new reading curriculum, a coach can observe and meet with six teams of four educators each.

We have witnessed the additive effect of coaching in a team-based context where teaching and learning are on full display. It is more possible for educators to observe one another teach, ask questions in real time, and collaboratively discuss student outcomes associated with particular changes in instructional practice. This is especially true for preservice and recently inducted teachers who have multiple professional educators from whom they can learn, making the need for external, drop-in coaches less obvious in team-based contexts.

To address challenges and opportunities associated with professional learning and coaching in team-based staffing models, many of our partner schools have adopted at least one of the following strategies:

- **Cede earmarked whole-school planning time to educator teams:** Several schools with which we partner have early release one day a week (or a month). Historically, the site-level leader used that time for whole-school professional learning. After introducing team-based staffing, they retained 25 percent of the days for whole-school programming but empowered educator teams to use the other 75 percent in ways that they thought would best advance their professional growth and student outcomes.

- **Utilize the Distributed Expertise Staffing Matrix to identify areas for personalized professional learning:** Every team that we work with during our Summer Institute for Educator Teams completes the Distributed Expertise Staffing Matrix. Trust and the capacity for vulnerability must be earned before this tool is especially helpful, but when educators are able to honestly reflect on their areas of strength and areas where the team can identify collective skill gaps, it is possible to become more strategic about personalized professional learning.
- **Deploy coaches strategically:** Across dozens of schools, we have seen coaches (math and reading specialists, induction coaches, professional development specialists) deployed more strategically. Their schedules are designed so they can both observe multiple teams operating in their areas of expertise and attend collaborative planning time with multiple educator teams each week.

Coordination of the extended team. Members of extended teams often include community educators (e.g., tutors, project-based mentors), paraeducators, student-facing specialists (e.g., school resource officers, special educators, speech-language pathologists, social workers), and educator coaches (e.g., literacy coaches, math specialists). When deployed strategically to complement core educator teams, extended team members can have an outsized impact on both educators and students. However, as any classroom teacher who has welcomed another adult into the learning space knows, coordinating multiple adults is no small feat.

In traditional staffing models, sometimes it is more difficult to integrate other educators than it would be with a team-based approach. For example, if a paraeducator is to be shared among four teachers on a grade level, there might be a fair bit of strategy involved as to how to best deploy this person. By day of the week? By time of the day? In a team-based approach, less coordination may be required at the school level. In this example, perhaps those four teachers comprise a single educator team, and the paraeducator is simply assigned to that team as a *core* team member. The team is empowered to determine how to best deploy that person in the learning space, and that strategy can change over time without scheduling difficulties. Similar efficiencies might be found when integrating external tutors or other community educators. Rather than trying to coordinate four teachers, a school-level leader might need to work with only a single representative from the team.

It gets more complicated, however, when extended teammates are shared among or across educator teams. This may be necessary for budgetary reasons, or even because the educators are working across schools. In these cases, care must be taken when constructing school-level schedules to ensure that shared, extended teammates can be doing the right work, with the right people, at the right time. For example, if an elementary paraeducator is shared across a pair of teams and is helping to deliver intervention support during the English language arts (ELA) block, the schedule is designed so those instructional blocks happen at different times on each team. The same can be said for when collaborative planning times occur across teams. There are many advantages to having staggered planning times, including the opportunity for coaches or site-level leaders to join more planning sessions.

To address challenges associated with coordinating extended team members in team-based contexts, schools with whom we've partnered have started small and then scaled up. In the case of extended team members, consider easy, uncomplicated ways to start the work. For example, rather than trying to build the perfect schedule that will allow speech-language pathologists to integrate with every team for which they have a student on the caseload, instead set the goal of having those specialists embed with one team for two hours every day for a week, or join each team's collaborative planning time once a month.

Planning time. The most important job of site-level leaders implementing team-based staffing models is to ensure that every educator team has sufficient time to plan together. Their second most important job is to help ensure that time is well spent. In chapter 5, we described how school leaders have figured out how to create more collaborative planning time for educator teams. Here, we provide insight into how teams effectively use the time that they have.

In most contexts, there is a tremendous amount of oversight in how each instructional minute is spent. Educators often have detailed, to-the-minute lesson plans, and nearly every observation occurs during instruction. This all seems logical. However, it does raise the interesting question of what would happen if educator planning time were similarly considered. In collaborative planning, the stakes for using that time are high. Ineffective minutes are not accrued by single educators, but rather by all participants, sometimes as many as four to eight educators.

In the context of the protected collaborative planning time that must accompany team-based staffing models, it is important that educators own that time and plan it strategically. To that end, we have collected several samples of what high-quality, collaborative planning agendas might look like. The details of these agendas are less important than several larger points, including the following:

- Teams should prepare agendas before their time together, and site-level leaders should value that preplanning.
- Every collaborative planning agenda always contains a few standing items (e.g., personal pulse checks, quick wins from the team, learners whom the team needs to celebrate, learners about whom there are concerns).
- There is a clear facilitator for the meeting. For teams that include a lead teacher, the person in that role may be the natural facilitator, or perhaps that job rotates among the team, as is often the case for teams without a formal lead teacher.
- There are a handful of focus areas that repeat on some predictable basis, including insights from extended team members (e.g., a monthly visit from the speech-language pathologist), student groups based on data/student work, a focus on families, and an upcoming content preview.

The substance of a collaborative planning agenda for an educator team will naturally vary as a function of the frequency with which the team meets, the length of the meetings, the complexity of the team, and the time of year. Above all, it is important that site-level leaders help to communicate how precious collaborative planning time is and share that understanding with the educator teams.

To ensure that collaborative planning time is well spent when moving to team-based staffing models, partner schools have adopted at least one of the following strategies:

- **Running cloud-based planning agendas:** Thanks to the power of shared, cloud-based documents, it is possible for every team to keep a running collaborative planning agenda and share it with site-based leaders. We have seen schools find success with creating a single, shared document, with each successive agenda added at the top. As a site-based leader, it is then possible to save all the links to each team's running agenda for easy access and reference.

- **Use of planning time in evaluation rubrics:** If we believe that we get what we measure and collaborative planning time is critical to the success of team-based staffing models, then it would make sense to add effective use of planning time to updated educator evaluation instruments.

Systems Associated with School Operations

Taking attendance and locating students. Knowing that two of the strengths of team-based staffing models are that students are regrouped throughout the day and educator teams are able to adjust the daily schedule to best meet the needs of their learners, pinpointing where a student should be at any moment can be a challenge. This is especially true if what used to be four individual classrooms is now considered one learning space and students are equally likely to be in any of those four rooms.

From a student's perspective, they are provided a personalized schedule that tells them where they need to be when. Depending on the frequency of the adjustment, these schedules might be posted on the board or class website (when changes are happening more frequently) or printed for the students' reference (for less frequent changes). We have found that even students in early elementary grades can manage dynamic schedules, often with the use of pictures. But like all systems, these must be thoughtfully introduced, strategically scaffolded, and frequently practiced.

From an educator's perspective, knowing each student's location at any given moment can be more challenging, especially if that information is asked for on the fly (e.g., the front office calls for a student). The same systems that exist for students also help teachers, but they may be less readily accessible. For example, if students have personalized printed schedules that change every four weeks, students quickly internalize where to be and when, but teachers may not know exactly where a particular learner is from memory.

Even a task as seemingly easy as taking attendance can be challenging in a team-based staffing model. Rather than having a set roster that remains the same all year, students may be in new groups as frequently as every day. Even if educators know where each student should be and when, registering that information in the formal attendance reporting structures can add a layer of work.

To address these challenges, we have seen schools implementing team-based staffing models adopt at least one of the following strategies:

- **W3 rosters:** Each team draws up, and shares with the front office, a "who/where/when (W3)" roster that identifies where each student should be at what time. These are often shared documents or spreadsheets. Each team updates its W3 roster as needed (daily, weekly, every several weeks) as part of its natural planning work drawing up student groups. And because it is in a shared document, the front office immediately has the most up-to-date record of where students should be and when.
- **Identified job:** Some teams designate a specific educator to be the "knower of the roster." That way, rather than every educator needing to know and have access to a detailed account of where every student should be and when, one person can be the single point of contact for the front office or any questions related to where students are learning. They may also be a person who has the responsibility for transcribing attendance tracked in informal ways (e.g., shared spreadsheets) into more formal systems once a day.
- **Ask the students:** It turns out that the students themselves are very good at knowing the location of most of their peers. We've found that rather than building and maintaining formal systems, the question can simply be turned over to the students: "Where is Marcia M. right now?" "Oh, she's in the Rainforest room with Mr. Saenz and Ms. Thompson."

Tracking instructional minutes. Related to recording attendance and knowing student whereabouts is the question of tracking instructional minutes. Many states require schools to keep track of time spent in specific subject areas. In addition, as per federal law, schools are required to track the number of minutes of services identified in students' individualized education programs (IEPs) and time for those students who receive English-language development support. In the one-teacher, one-classroom model, especially with pull-out support, it is relatively easy to track all the time-based requirements.

With more inclusive, team-based staffing models, however, tracking specific minutes becomes substantially more difficult. For example, we have high schools that have turned off their bells, and what once was four, sixty-minute periods of biology, English, world history, and algebra I are now given to teams of four educators as a block of 240 minutes. The team is empowered to build strategic schedules based on the students' learning needs, the curricula, and known educator factors (e.g., the biology teacher will be gone Thursday and Friday at the National Science Teaching conference). Sometimes the team builds a schedule that looks like four sixty-minute periods, but sometimes they offer one subject a day for 240 minutes and the students rotate through four classes over four days. Tracking instructional minutes becomes even more confusing on days where students spend the entire four hours working on interdisciplinary projects that span all four subjects.

To address these challenges, we have seen schools adopt at least one of the following strategies:

- **Timekeeper:** In much the same way that educator teams identify a person responsible for knowing where students are physically located and taking attendance, some teams also name a person responsible for maintaining records of the total number of instructional minutes, broken into the necessary categories. There may be formal software solutions to help with this, but many schools simply use shared spreadsheets.
- **Software solutions:** It's likely that your school is already using software solutions that might help teams keep track of instructional minutes. The same software that could be used for dynamically grouping learners and taking attendance should also be able to handle maintaining a record of the total instructional minutes.

Access to data. In a one-teacher, one-classroom staffing model, each educator typically has access to all the student's data in the subject areas being taught. In elementary contexts, this almost always translates to twenty to thirty students. Around report card time, homeroom teachers may receive grades from a handful of other teachers in areas like physical education or music, but they typically don't have much visibility into what is happening in other classes. The lack of shared access to data is even starker in secondary schools, where students have multiple teachers throughout the day. This all makes sense: this staffing model was designed for siloing, and student data are not an exception.

In team-based staffing models, it is imperative that all educators on the core team have access to the full set of data associated with each learner. Critically, these are not just academic data, but also whole-child measures, including things such as sense of belonging, personal preferences, and growth on broader outcomes such as self-direction and curiosity. Although the core team needs access to all of a learner's data, educators on the extended team likely do not, and for privacy reasons, they should not have access to everything. Instead, there must be systems and structures that allow the educator team to provide the right data to the right educators at the right time, with a general recommendation for conservatism. For example, if project-based mentors from business and industry are meeting with students once a week over the course of a unit, they may need to know how students are performing relative to only a narrow set of related standards or broader skills, and even then maybe only areas of strength and areas on which to focus the next rounds of feedback.

To address the challenges associated with sharing data, we have seen schools that are implementing team-based staffing models consider a data-sharing matrix. To create guardrails around who should have access to which types of data, some schools draft or revise a data-sharing matrix at the beginning of each school year. A working group comprising members of teams from across the school creates this shared resource for the school, which lists types of data specific to the school and clearly identifies which educators should have access to each type.

CONCLUDING THOUGHTS ON SYSTEMS AND STRUCTURES FOR TEAMS

The examples described in this chapter represent some of the most frequently cited structures and systems that school leaders must navigate when transitioning to team-based staffing models. Again, the point in categorizing them by systems affecting students/families, educators, and school operations is not to create a punch list of systems you need to change. Rather, we offer these examples as a framework and a starting point to begin to identify, interrogate, and in many cases change systems and structures that are in potential conflict with a team-based approach to staffing.

In the preceding few pages, we have provided examples of strategies, workarounds, and concrete resources that school leaders have put into place as they have stood up team-based staffing models in their contexts. Many of these solutions are temporary at best, and in several cases, they end up creating more work for educators. Ultimately, as more school systems transition to team-based staffing models and we network together, it will be possible to create greater demand for better-aligned products and to advocate for changes to systems and structures that currently reinforce traditional models of staffing schools.

In chapter 8, you will take all the things that you have learned about launching your first team up to now and consider what it will take to build more teams at your school. This will require more systems to shift at greater scale, including educator teams, schedules, learning spaces, and all the considerations in this chapter. The next chapter will give you some considerations for doing this.

CHAPTER 8

Scaling Team-Based Staffing

Principal Krista Adams at Stevenson Elementary had a plan for launching team-based staffing at her school. She would begin with a single third-grade team and then add a team in each successive year to support the next grade level up. Krista wanted to create the time and space for slow, durable change to occur. However, what happened over the course of the first year surprised her. Educators on the third-grade team were thriving and providing engaging, personalized learning experiences for students—and this happened during the year of rolling, pandemic-related school closures. The third-grade team talked informally with other educators on campus about the sense of support that they felt from each other and how they were able to meet learners' varied needs in ways that they never had before. It was not long before educators began to approach Krista asking if they, too, could be members of teams, and as a result, Stevenson moved forward the following year with some form of teaming in every grade level.

Things progressed differently at Westwood High School, a comprehensive ninth- to twelfth-grade school with nearly 3,600 students. There, team-based staffing scaled at a slower rate. School leadership started with three ninth-grade teams, serving about 270 of the nearly 900 freshmen. The first educator teams were successful in better meeting the needs of students, and core class pass rates improved. Principal Chris Gilmore recognized the need to build an administrative team that could better support the move to team-based staffing and keep the educator team structure roughly the same in year two. In the third year of implementation, Westwood added three more teams, which resulted in all ninth graders at Westwood being supported by educator teams. Gilmore, other school leaders, and team-based educators continued to refine the structure of the ninth-grade teams over the next three years and piloted a few small teams in tenth grade. During that time, school and district leaders also created the longer-term vision for college and career academy pathways staffed by educator teams for students in grades 10–12, which continues to shape Westwood's *why for teaming* and next steps. Six years into the school's journey of launching team-based models, about half of Westwood's students are supported by teams, with more to be added over time.

This chapter is, by design, intended for leaders who have successfully launched their first team and are interested in scaling team-based staffing at their school site. How quickly you scale and what steps you take next will vary depending on your school and community. The content provided in chapters 2 through 7 still have utility and will be a helpful reread as you expand the number of educator teams. That said, there are new challenges and opportunities associated with moving from having just one team to implementing team-based staffing more broadly. Nearly every school leader with whom we have worked crafted an initial plan for launching and scaling team-based staffing models at their site and then adjusted those plans over time based on conversations with educators, families, students, and other community members.

Rather than introduce a new framework for scaling team-based staffing models, we instead present our insights and lessons learned from school partners under the headings from the preceding chapters, with small twists. For example, as you deepen your implementation, you don't need to identify your *why for teaming*—you need to refine it. Or, if your first team has already figured out how to create more collaborative and flexible learning spaces, your new challenge is what to do when you need to find space for multiple educator teams. This chapter highlights a few lessons learned–and questions that you may ask yourself–as you continue your journey from launching team-based staffing models to scaling them at your site.

REFINING YOUR *WHY FOR TEAMING*

In chapter 2, we challenged you to identify your *why for teaming* and associated goals for improved educator and student outcomes. It's entirely possible that your overarching *why* hasn't changed since you designed and launched your first team. However, you probably have new insights, and you are likely ready to refine your *why*, especially as you contemplate scaling. You will do this in many ways, but we'd encourage you to look at your data, think about other major initiatives, and ask those closest to the work for their insights.

Look at Your Data

Imagine leaders from a large comprehensive high school who originally identified the need to improve student attendance as their *why for teaming* and consequently set out to build team-based learning environments for a subset of students. Their hope was that students would experience a greater sense of belonging and, in turn, be more likely to come to school. A year later, students served by educator teams have higher attendance rates on average, but gaps persist across demographic lines. Should these leaders scale teaming at the school? What refinements should they make to build on their successes?

Here are a few data-related questions that you may ask yourself as you refine your own *why for teaming*:

- Look at your data and respond to what you see. What are your early data telling you about improved educator and student outcomes? What is working? What surprises you? Where do you want to see improvements in the next one to two years?
- Determine what additional data you need to collect and analyze. What data do you need to measure to monitor growth toward the improvements you seek? As an example, do you need new student or educator surveys to measure the outcomes that you care about most?
- Consider what was important to you, your educators, and your school community when you first launched teams. Are those priorities still the most important to you today? What new priorities have emerged?

Alignment with Other Initiatives

When designing your first team and navigating the change management process, you may have considered the intersection of team-based staffing and other strategic initiatives or major investments of the school or school system. You also started small—likely with one or two first teams—which did not require you to think about the long-term implications for alignment between all the initiatives in place at your school. When you are contemplating scaling, it is a great time to consider longer-term alignment. For example, if school leaders have made a commitment to personalized, competency-based learning (PCBL) and are considering increasing the number of teams at their site, they will need to think through how team-based staffing interacts with PCBL. In this case, the competency-based nature of the curriculum might unlock an ability to build educator teams that support multiaged groups of learners, something that the leaders may not have initially considered in their first year of launching team-based models.

Here are a few of the most common initiatives on which schools have been simultaneously focused as we support them in implementing team-based staffing models. In addition to suggesting how educator teaming might align with these initiatives, we offer a few questions worthy of asking as you increase the number of educators and students in team-based models.

Common Simultaneous Initiative with Teaming

High-Quality Instructional Materials

Effective teaching requires high-quality instructional materials that provide structured yet flexible learning experiences to meet diverse student needs. Looking across various examples of high-quality instructional materials (HQIM), one notices that, at their core, each involves teaching students in whole groups, small groups, and individually. There are important questions about the role of educator teams in maximizing the impact of HQIM and supporting differentiated instruction. Consider the following:

- Do educator teams allow you to better support those various learning modalities? Which educators on the teams are best suited for which types of instruction? Are the answers the same for all content areas?
- To the degree that you are also engaged in implementation coaching around HQIM, how might your team-based structure and educator coplanning time allow more effective coaching and support around instruction? As you scale to more teams, what impact will that have on these supports?

Portraits of a Graduate/Learner

Interdisciplinary units, project-based learning, and authentic assessment—among other learner-centered approaches—center on the skills and mindsets often represented in portraits of a graduate. Consider the following when thinking about the intersections of portraits of a graduate and team-based staffing:

- How might educator teams be able to codesign and codeliver this type of learning experience consistently and with quality?
- By nature of the team-based approach, members of educator teams model for students' communication, collaboration, and other portrait-aligned skills in ways that are very difficult to do in a one-teacher, one-classroom model. How might educator teams explicitly and implicitly model specific skills found in many portraits?

College and Career Pathways/Academies

College and career academies are a growing reform effort in high schools across the United States.[1] At Westwood and Skyline High Schools, leaders are using team-based staffing as a way to better support students in a specific academy. For instance, there are tenth- and eleventh-grade teams in the Health Sciences Academy. Complemented by the career focus of the academy, academic teachers and career and technical education teachers are able to plan interdisciplinary units to deliver to their shared rosters of students. In this case, scaling team-based models has helped deepen the work of implementing college and career academies. The following are a few considerations for college and career pathways and educator teams:

- How broadly are we defining the educator team? Are there others, especially community educators from business and industry, who could be playing a more substantial role on the team?
- How might internship experiences, and the community educators providing them, stay connected as extended team members? As you scale team-based models, how will you coordinate requests of the community so as to not overwhelm or confuse them?

New Teacher Induction Programs

New teacher induction programs play a critical role in supporting and retaining novice educators. Educator teams have the potential to provide more embedded, day-to-day support while also distributing instructional responsibilities so that novice educators have responsibilities that match their expertise. As schools consider how team-based staffing intersects with new teacher induction, key questions emerge, such as:

- Did we place novice teachers on teams? If so, what were their roles and responsibilities? How did those differ (or not) relative to novices in traditional staffing models?
- What specific expertise or training might be needed by more senior members of the teams on which novices are placed?
- Does placing novices on teams reduce or eliminate the need for support for new teachers coming from the school system? If so, is it possible to redistribute resources so that more are going directly to the educator teams on which novice teachers are placed?

Ask Those Closest to the Work

Finally, as you are refining your *why for teaming* and look to scale educator teams on your site, it is imperative that you engage those closest to the work, including the team-based educators and the students whom they support. You could formally survey them, but we've found small focus groups to be even more powerful. Regardless of the method, you may consider asking questions like the following:

- What impact has the team-based approach had on our students?
- What impact has the team-based approach had on educators on teams?
- What impact has the team-based approach had on educators not on teams?
- What impact has the team-based approach had on our school?
- What impact has the team-based approach had on you?
- What surprised you most about being a member of an educator team this year?
- If you had to name one or two things that being a member of an educator team made *better* this year, what would those be?
- If you had to name one or two things that being a member of an educator team made *worse* or *more challenging* this year, what would those be?
- We described our *why for teaming* as *X*. In your experience this year, did *X* happen? How do you know?

- What should we keep the same for our team-based model next year?
- What adjustments should we consider for our team-based model next year?

Taken together, your data, alignment with other important initiatives, and perspectives of people closest to the implementation of your first team-based model will help you to refine your *why for teaming*. Having a clear *why* is imperative when launching your first team, but it is perhaps even more important when scaling team-based models at your site because more members of your community will be directly affected, and you will likely encounter more people interested in preserving the status quo.

ASSESSING READINESS FOR SCALE

In chapter 3, we carefully considered how to navigate the change from traditional staffing models to a team-based approach. Assuming that your *why for teaming* remains strong, the associated outcomes are trending positively, and your community is asking questions about what's next, you are likely thinking about scaling the number of educator teams at your site.

When considering your readiness for scale, you will want to (1) assess the current state of your school's enabling conditions for scaling team-based staffing and (2) assess the site's readiness to scale. The *enabling conditions* are external and structural factors that contribute to change, while *readiness for change* is primarily about attitudes and psychological preparedness.[2]

Assessing Enabling Conditions for Scale

Your *why for teaming*, the master schedule, redesigned learning spaces, and any infrastructural changes made as a result of your first teams are all examples of enabling conditions. Once you decide to scale teaming at your site, here are a few other enabling conditions that we have found to be especially important:

- **Leadership support:** Leaders, at the both the school and school-system levels, must be champions of educator teams and help remove barriers, enabling teams to thrive.
- **Adequate time for teams:** As a result of intentional master scheduling, educators working on teams have adequate shared time—both for planning and instruction—to craft and deliver learning experiences, analyze data, and dynamically group and regroup students.

- **Empowerment:** Educators on teams feel empowered to make decisions that best meet the needs of their shared roster of learners, and the right guardrails are in place to allow this level of educator autonomy.
- **Professional learning:** Team-based educators have access to professional learning that allows them to improve their practice both as individuals and as a collective unit. For example, as individuals, educators may focus on developing new skills to meet the needs of particular learners on their roster or take on more ambitious forms of teaching like interdisciplinary units or advanced techniques in the science of reading. With respect to operating as a collective unit, educators may pursue professional learning on topics like improving team dynamics or strategies for better deploying teammates based on multiple forms of data.

How would you rate your ability to support each of these four conditions for scaling team-based staffing models at your site? It is unlikely that after a year of piloting a single team, a school will be strong in all these aspects. However, before committing to scaling, you should have a plan for deepening your commitment to each of these conditions and any others that would be especially important in your particular context.

Assessing Readiness to Scale

While you are assessing your enabling conditions for scale, you should also assess your school community's readiness to scale. Here, we think of community as students, educators, families, and other external school partners, such as local industry. Community readiness is an important indicator as to whether the change will sustain. In 2007, researchers Daniel Holt and colleagues published an instrument that assesses employee's "readiness for organizational change at an individual level."[3] We have adapted their instrument to assess a *community's* readiness for change. Readiness for change is influenced by individuals who believe the following:

- They are capable of implementing a proposed change.
- The proposed change is appropriate for the organization.
- The leaders [of the organization] are committed to the proposed change.
- The proposed change is beneficial to organizational members.

Here are four questions, aligned with the aforementioned characteristics, that we believe are worth asking as you are assessing your community's readiness to scale team-based staffing. You can find specific protocol questions to accompany each section on our Authors' Page.

Does the community feel that they are capable of scaling team-based staffing? Whether your community, specifically additional educators, feel capable of implementing team teaching is one of the first areas that you might explore as you assess your school's readiness. "Change confidence," also known as "change self-efficacy," "refers to the extent to which one feels that he or she has or does not have the skills and is or is not able to execute the tasks and activities that are associated with the implementation of the prospective change."[4]

Does the community feel that team teaching is appropriate to scale at the school site? If educators, families, and stakeholders do not see a clear rationale for scaling, concern about schoolwide scale is more likely. This is why your *why for teaming* needs to be clearly defined to all key actors early and clearly. Another way to think about appropriateness is, "Does your community perceive a need for scale?" This readiness condition focuses on "the extent to which one feels that there are or are not legitimate reasons and needs for the prospective change."[5] This is the time to refer back to your refined *why for teaming* and ensure that it is properly communicated.

Does the community feel that school- and system-level leaders are committed to scaling team-based staffing models? The commitment of school and system-level leadership "refers to the extent to which one feels that the organization's leadership and management are or are not committed to and support or do not support implementation of the prospective change."[6] Some members of the community, especially experienced teachers, may see changes in schools as pendulum swings that go back and forth. Some teachers might even hope that they can ride out changes at the school. Clear commitment of school and system-level leadership underscores that scaling team-based staffing models aligns with the larger vision, they will provide consistent support, and they themselves will change their day-to-day actions as new staffing models are implemented.

Do members of the community see personal and school-level benefits to scaling team-based models? A final consideration should be given to whether members of the community see both personal and school-level benefits to implementing team teaching. Of course, there will be trade-offs associated with scaling the model, and there will not always be positive sentiments about the change, but that does not diminish the need for members of the community to feel the anticipated benefits—especially educators and students, and their families.

BUILDING YOUR NEXT EDUCATOR TEAMS

As you think about building your next set of educator teams, the same considerations that you used to select your first teams still apply. What is different is the context in which educators are making the move to teaming. Your first teams likely included your innovators—educators who were willing to take a bold step before an example was shown to them in your building or there was proof that the change would work. Now you have real-life examples of how teaming can work in your particular context and lessons learned to draw upon, and ideally, can build momentum and excitement behind your efforts.

As you begin to scale team-based models at your site, your next teams will likely include early adopters and members of the early majority, whom Everett Rogers identifies as those who may be willing to adopt an innovation once change is in motion. Here are some questions that you may want to ask as you involve more educators when scaling team-based staffing at your site.

Nurture and Support Team Health

- *What learning might school leaders and educator teams need to do about team development, dynamics, and culture?* Educators sometimes hold misperceptions about what healthy team functioning looks like. For example, many often believe that an effective team always agrees when in fact, healthy, productive conflict is a key indicator of team health. Provide opportunities to learn about team development and culture.
- *What structures will you proactively put into place to nurture team culture across the school year?* Highly effective teams are built, not born, and educators who have worked in only one-teacher, one-classroom models will likely need support in developing the habits of healthy teams. We offer resources to get started on establishing team health on our Authors' Page.

Make Adjustments to First Teams

- *Will you keep existing teams together or split them apart to create new teams?* Many school leaders initially think that splitting up team members makes good sense as a way to spread innovation. Well-functioning educator teams, however, will often push back against this because they want to stay together. Having a few very high-functioning teams can benefit the newer teams because of the strong example that they provide, and those teams often act as incubators for new ideas.

- *Do you need to make any changes to your first teams? Do you have any teams that just didn't gel and could benefit from one or two new teammates? Do you have any teachers who retired, resigned, or want to opt out?* While these scenarios may not sound ideal, transformative levels of change are not for everyone, and continuing to rework team composition until you get the right balance is a natural part of the process.

Decide How Many New Teams to Add

- *Are you adding one to two more teams, or are you going schoolwide with teaming?* Knowing how many teachers you plan to transition to team-based staffing will help you select the next group of educators from which you can compose your next set of teams.
- *What data can you provide about what you've learned to date?* Those in the early majority will be expecting data about what's working for students and educators in team-based models in your particular context.
- *Is there motivation and excitement for team-based models among educators? Students? Families?* If so, like Krista Adams from this chapter's introduction, you may want to capitalize on the momentum and add even more teams than you were anticipating.
- *If you plan to expand broadly, are there educators on staff who might be happier making a shift to another campus without a team-based model?* Every school leader with whom we've worked has described staff members who resist change. Depending on your context (e.g., the number of open positions, the specifics of a union contract, and the size of your school system), you may not be in a position to encourage those educators to find other positions, and you may want to add teams more slowly. Top-down mandates of "Everyone is teaming" rarely go well. At some point, the culture will shift and team-based staffing will become the expectation, but building that culture may take time.

Iterate on Team Composition and Shared Rosters

- *How might the composition of the team change as a function of the age or grade level of students?* At Westwood High School, for example, team-based staffing started in the ninth grade, where all freshmen were supported by teams of four educators, including a career and technical education teacher. As students move to college and career pathways, educator teams are smaller and become more specialized.
- *What adjustments will you make to the number of students supported by your educator teams?* Some schools start with a smaller number of students in the first year (eighty, for example) and then move to a larger shared roster (perhaps 120) in the second year. A larger roster of students often equates to more team members, providing increased flexibility for the educator team to use dynamic student grouping.

Identify Opportunities for New Roles and Advancement

- *What are the opportunities for new roles on teams that are emerging as you increase the number of teams at your school?* Might you be ready to add a new special educator as an extended team member across two teams? What about community educators? Or lead teachers?
- *What advancement opportunities might you offer educators?* For example, perhaps a student teacher is ready for a full-time role on the team, a para-educator has been taking coursework and can take on a certified role, or a team teacher is ready to be a lead teacher. Consider who may be ready for the next step and extend opportunities accordingly.

The Transformational Teacher Leader Role

ASU Preparatory Academy is adopting a role similar to the Teacher Executive Designer at Kyrene de las Manitas Innovation Academy called *Transformational Teacher Leader (TTL)*. The TTL is a position designed to bridge the gap between traditional teaching roles and school leadership. TTLs are tasked with a dual responsibility: to coach, mentor, and lead a set of educators and to be directly accountable for the outcomes of the students in their caseload. TTLs are similar to assistant principals in responsibility, authority, and compensation, but they are closer to the day-to-day routine of teaching and learning.

Empower Educators in Hiring and Amplifying Educator Voice

What role will educators play in selecting their teams or hiring a new teammate? Ideally, as teaming scales in your building, educators will have more say in the hiring process, as they will have a deeper understanding of the distributed expertise that they need to strengthen their particular team. We've also observed that when educators have a voice in deciding who joins their team, they assume more responsibility for the new teammate's success.

How might you empower educators who are currently members of teams to share their experience with other educators? Some school leaders create opportunities for team members to present at staff meetings. Educators who are considering the shift to team-based models will want to hear from those who are doing the work. Encourage educators to be honest about their experience and answer questions directly. Hiring substitutes to cover classes for traditionally staffed teachers to observe in team-based environments can also be an effective way to help them get a better sense of what might be possible in team-based models.

MASTER SCHEDULING FOR GREATER FLEXIBILITY WHILE ACCOMMODATING COMPLEXITY

Framed positively, master schedules are the great puzzles that school leaders get to solve at least once a year. As discussed in chapter 5, team-based staffing makes a hard puzzle even harder. Having more educator teams often means adding more complexity when scheduling extended team members such as specials teachers (e.g., art, physical education, music) or when navigating elective offerings.

When creating master schedules, elementary school leaders often spread each team's intervention blocks across the school day. As highlighted in table 8.1, the reading and math intervention blocks are offered at different times for each team. This allows extended team members, like content coaches and special educators, to push in with multiple teams over a single day. When extended team members join core teams, they bring specialized expertise and lower educator-to-student ratios for strategic sets of learners.

In secondary schools, more educator teams, especially across multiple grade levels, create complexities in the master schedule around balancing elective choices and preserving large, contiguous blocks of time where the same team of educators share the same roster of students.

TABLE 8.1 Sample elementary schedule that allows extended team members to strategically join multiple teams during a single day

Team 1	*Team 2*	*Team 3*
Family meeting	Family meeting	Family meeting
Content block 1	Math intervention *Paraeducator math specialist* *Academic interventionist*	Specials/planning
Content block 2	Content block 1	Math intervention *Paraeducator math specialist* *Academic interventionist*
Reading intervention *Reading specialist + high school literacy tutors*	Content block 2	Content block 1
Content block 3	Reading intervention *Reading specialist + high school literacy tutors*	Content block 2
Specials/planning	Content block 3	Reading intervention *Reading specialist + high school literacy tutors*
Math intervention *Paraeducator math specialist* *Academic interventionist*	Specials/planning	Content block 3

At Westwood High School, ninth-grade academy teams share instructional time for four periods of the day. In their initial years of teaming, all educator teams shared students for four consecutive class periods, which placed considerable constraints on the number of elective periods available to ninth-grade students. School leaders brainstormed possible solutions with educators. Team members suggested trying some two-period blocks of shared instructional time: for example, an educator team might have shared instructional time during the first two and last two periods of each day. The administrative team found that this provided more flexibility in their elective offerings and provided the unanticipated benefit of a "check in, check out" system with their students.

Whether in an elementary or secondary context, as the number of educators working in team-based models increases, so too does the complexity of master scheduling. Quite frankly, it is easier to let scheduling software design the master schedule to maximize efficiency and coverage. We have seen, however, that when communities desire outcomes related to connection, relationships, and greater learning, the investment in getting the master schedule right for multiple educator teams is worth it. A few questions that might inform your master schedules that include multiple educator teams could be the following:

- *Are there ways to work outside the typical schedule that might bring more flexibility?* For example, some schools have a "zero hour," where they offer band, choir, and other electives.
- *Are there fundamental shifts in scheduling that might create more flexibility in your master schedule?* For example, we have worked with high schools that shifted from six-period days to block scheduling. This change created more flexibility to accommodate team-based models by opening up two additional periods for electives, a ninety-minute block period each day for team and individual planning, and extended periods of time for students to engage in deeper and more personalized learning. Within a 4x4 block schedule, there are eight periods for academic courses as opposed to the typical six courses, making it easier for students to recover credit or access additional learning.
- *What are the priorities of the administrative team as you move into the next school year?* You considered your *why for teaming* and your priorities in year one. As a leadership team, revisit both and take the time to clearly articulate and align on what's most important to you in the next school year. How does your master schedule reflect those priorities?
- *What boutique programs or smaller classes may be affected by adding more educator teams?* As more teams get added, you'll likely need to reconsider whether the full-time employees being allocated to particular sections with low enrollment would be better deployed for educator teams.
- *What lessons did those who create the master schedule (such as registrars) learn by building the master schedule in year one?* Master schedule builders will likely have insights into how to streamline the schedule-building process as you scale the number of teams. You might also have your schedule builder talk with schedule builders from other schools who are also implementing team-based models in order to share insights with one another.

MOVING ALONG THE CONTINUUM OF LEARNING ENVIRONMENTS

As you add more teams across your school site, return to the Continuum of Learning Environments introduced in chapter 6. This tool can serve as a helpful guide as you think about how to best meet the space needs of your growing number of teams. It can also help provide direction for future investments in physical space redesign, furniture, and resources.

Often, the first educator team at a school gets access to spaces that allow greater collaboration and flexibility, such as rooms with movable walls (level 2 on the continuum). However, as the number of educator teams at a site increases, the number of these more flexible spaces stays the same. With more teams, you may actually find that as a school, you move backward on the continuum, and depending on how you allocate space, the team may feel less supported than they did initially with respect to access to flexible learning environments.

On the other hand, your first teams may have built so much interest and support from your community that people are ready to make investments in new spaces. We have seen enterprising school leaders use the success of their first teams to marshal investments from local funders, businesses, and parent-based organizations toward making improvements to the learning environments. Unlike other investments in education, which may take years to materialize or are hard to see, improvements to learning environments are often immediate and tangible.

As you scale team-based staffing at your site, consider how your spaces can best be designed for learners and allow the greatest amounts of flexibility. Here are a few items to reflect on based on lessons learned from teams as they moved from one to many teams within a school.

Designing New Learning Spaces and Learning Zones

- *What furniture, equipment, or new construction makes sense to invest in at this stage of your change process?* Are you ready to add glass windows or doors between classrooms? Replace existing furniture with new tables and chairs to support different learning environments?
- *Consider what new, larger spaces you are ready to create now that more educators and students will be working in teams.* Perhaps you are ready to rework your atrium, library, and cafeteria spaces to better support teaming.

- *Consider what new learning zones educators are ready to add within their existing learning spaces.* Perhaps more educators and students are ready for spaces like independent learning zones or research/exploration centers to support personalized learning.

Creating New Norms for Scale

As the number of teams increases, so does the demand for common space. Hallways may often be protected for team-specific uses, but other shared spaces across the school will likely be in higher demand and require a scheduling or reservation system to ensure equitable access for all teams.

As the number of students on teams increases, consider creating schoolwide shared norms for how students will move about learning spaces *across* the school building. In teaming, students will likely access learning spaces outside the immediate proximity of their teams on a more frequent basis than in the one teacher, one classroom paradigm. Shared language ensures that students don't have to learn new team-based systems and structures as they move from team to team.

As the number of students on teams grows, consider creating schoolwide shared norms for the levels of freedom (e.g., levels of autonomy) that students have *within* learning environments.

Work within existing systems for improving learning spaces. Most school systems have a rotating schedule for building improvements over a period of multiple years. If your school's facility improvements are coming up in the next cycle, be proactive in advocating for the type of updates and furniture that will support educator teams and the students that they support.

Redesigning Space for Multiple Uses

At Kyrene de las Manitas Innovation Academy, Principal Melissa Gradnigo redesigned an open space that accommodates up to 120 students and equipped it with science lab and media arts materials. There is also an open space where the performing arts educator can take students through movement activities. This use of space means that students can attend specials together with multiple educators. This provides the double impact of growing student relationships while also creating shared planning time for the core educator team. After school, a group of community educators uses the space for afterschool care.

SYSTEMS AND STRUCTURES FOR SUSTAINING TEAM-BASED MODELS

As described in chapter 7, a single educator team or two can be accommodated within the existing infrastructure of a school and school system for the most part. However, as sites move toward broader implementation or teaming schoolwide, the importance of having compatible systems and structures increases dramatically. Wider adoption of team-based models means that educators who are less tolerant of change and innovation will now be among the implementers, and they will not put up with clunky workarounds. Systems and structures need to move from scrappy solutions and "make it work" attitudes to formal systems that function at scale. While some of these systems may be within your locus of control at the site level, in our experience, most require change at the school-system level. For that reason, if you've made the commitment to scaling team-based models at your site, you should also have buy-in from systems-level leaders, as discussed earlier in this chapter.

The types of quick-fix solutions discussed in chapter 7 addressed the misalignment between team-based staffing models and most systems and structures in three broad categories: students and families, educators, and school systems. We use the same framework here, but these solutions are more complex, durable, and able to address challenges at scale. They often require change at the school-system level and may take significant time (and, in some cases, money) to enact.

Systems Associated with Students and Families

Community-facing marketing materials and experiences that highlight team-based models. Schools and school systems should develop collateral (e.g., videos, graphics, or brochures) that help communicate to families and other community members what team-based staffing models are and the school's *why for teaming*. Because most community members will have experienced only one-teacher, one-classroom models, it is important to help them shift their mental models for what teaching and learning can look like. Several of the schools with which we partner have started inviting parents and other community members to tour their team-based learning environments to see the models in action.

Team-based communication tools. As a sector, we need to build more family communication tools that start with the assumption that a team of educators supports each learner. This has been a long-standing need in the context of special education, and there are solutions that begin to address this issue, but current products are often overcomplicated or limit the type or number of educators who can share students. In the cases where a school or school system has a solution that can meet this need, training should be developed and/or default settings need to be reconfigured such that the starting assumption is that a team of educators shares each student and each educator can send and receive communication on behalf of the team. Specifically, there should be solutions for team-based email distribution lists from which to send and receive communications and team-based visibility into family communication logs.

Systems Associated with Educators

Create systems and structures for educators to drive their own professional learning. In the last several years, there has been an increasing focus on personalized professional learning for educators. Team-based staffing models, where educators can lean into their strengths and areas of interest, provide the perfect context for individuals to charter their own professional learning plans. Ideally, each educator could pursue a wide range of high-quality, competency-based personalized professional learning that would be recognized and rewarded by the school system. Tools like the team-level Distributed Expertise Staffing Matrix, which can be found on our Authors' Page, can help educators see how their personalized professional learning complements the combined expertise of the team.

Formally recognize and reward specializations and new roles in human resource systems. Ultimately, human resource (HR) systems should better reflect team-based approaches to staffing schools. School leaders should be able to signal specific hiring needs given the distributed expertise of the team, and the HR system should help match candidates with those open roles. For example, a site leader may be looking for a lower-elementary teacher with expertise in the science of reading, family communication, and data analysis. The HR system could provide a level of visibility into candidates who have expertise in those areas. Relatedly, as the number of educator teams increase, it may be necessary to add new, formal roles to HR systems. These may be roles that were piloted within the first team-based model (e.g., lead teacher, specialized paraeducator) but could now have specific job descriptions and salary bands that would likely require approval from the governing board. This is work that could happen before the first team launches; however, we have found it powerful to first pilot these roles to inform job descriptions and identify educators who can help champion the new positions.

Systems Associated with School Operations

Build student information systems around learners, not classes. There are some early products that fundamentally change the architecture of how each student's data are managed. These solutions balance well-warranted privacy concerns with accessibility of the right data by the right educators at the right time, all in one place.

Replace seat-time-based with competency-based learning. The anachronistic nature of seat-time-based learning is on full display as educators working on teams become more interdependent and learning becomes more interdisciplinary. An obvious solution is competency- or mastery-based learning. As the number of educator teams increases at a school site, educators often begin to question some of the other systems that are part of the traditional grammar of schooling (e.g., age-graded groupings).

Actualizing this set of recommendations would require significant investments of time and money. Some of these changes could happen at the site level, but most require changes at the level of the school-system, state, or service provider (e.g., the student information system provider). Justifying the level of investment needed to bring about these sorts of changes requires increased demand from school sites. This happens when a site moves from a single educator team to schoolwide teaming. But it also happens when multiple schools within the same system implement strategic school staffing models. The greatest opportunity for change comes when multiple school systems network to request similar changes to the underlying educational infrastructure, which is not aligned with team-based staffing models as it currently exists.

Our goal at the Next Education Workforce initiative is to catalyze and support educational leaders to design new team-based staffing models, support implementation, and help build a network of innovative educators who will collectively define and foster a new grammar of schooling.

CONCLUSION

This book represents our best understanding of the key actions that school leaders can take to launch and scale successful team-based staffing models in their contexts. Drawing from lessons learned from the past eight years, the guidance in this text is a summation of the best practices that we have learned from the pioneering and innovative group of schools and school leaders who set out to do this work before any examples existed. Today, we are all able to learn from their pathbreaking models. We hope that tomorrow, the next group of schools and school leaders will learn from you.

We also hope that this text has been helpful as you design and launch your first team-based staffing models, and we look forward to learning with and from you. We began this book by sharing our belief that for school to be *worth doing*, all students should have access to—and enjoy equitable outcomes from—deeper and more personalized learning experiences. To make that work *doable*, teachers should be staffed as teams of educators with distributed expertise who share the same roster of students. We hope that the actions described in this text will help make school more worth doing for your students and more doable for you and your fellow educators.

Notes

Introduction

1. David F. Labaree, "The Dynamic Tension at the Core of the Grammar of Schooling," *Phi Delta Kappan* 103, no. 2 (2021): 28–32, https://doi.org/10.1177/00317217211051141.
2. Center for Evaluation and Education Policy Analysis, "Trends in Enrollment and Completion in US Teacher Preparation Programs, 2009–2022," *CEEPA Blog*, March 1, 2024, https://ceepablog.wordpress.com/2024/03/01/trends-in-enrollment-and-completion-in-us-teacher-preparation-programs-2009-2022/; National Center for Education Statistics (NCES), "NCES Releases New Data on School Enrollment for 2023," press release, December 13, 2023, https://nces.ed.gov/whatsnew/press_releases/12_13_2023.asp; National Center for Education Statistics (NCES), *Characteristics of Public School Teachers* (Washington, DC: US Department of Education, 2023), https://nces.ed.gov/programs/coe/pdf/2023/clr_508.pdf.
3. Education Week Research Center, *Teaching Profession in Crisis: National Teacher Survey* (Bethesda, MD: Editorial Projects in Education, 2024), https://www.edweek.org/research-center/reports/teaching-profession-in-crisis-national-teacher-survey.
4. National Education Association (NEA), "NEA Survey: Massive Staff Shortages in Schools Leading to Educator Burnout; Alarming Number of Educators Are Considering Leaving the Profession," press release, January 31, 2024, https://www.nea.org/about-nea/media-center/press-releases/nea-survey-massive-staff-shortages-schools-leading-educator-burnout-alarming-number-educators; National Center for Education Statistics (NCES), "Eight Percent of Public School Teachers Left Teaching in 2021, a Rate Unchanged Since Last Measured in 2012," press release, December 13, 2023, https://nces.ed.gov/whatsnew/press_releases/12_13_2023.asp.
5. Desiree Carver-Thomas and Linda Darling-Hammond, *Teacher Turnover: Why It Matters and What We Can Do About It* (Palo Alto, CA: Learning Policy Institute, 2017), https://learningpolicyinstitute.org/sites/default/files/product-files/Teacher_Turnover_REPORT.pdf.
6. Axsium Group, "What Is Workforce Design?," February 15, 2022, https://axsiumgroup.com/what-is-workforce-design/.
7. Ann Cotton, *The Seven Steps of Effective Workforce Planning*, Human Capital Management Series (Washington, DC: IBM Center for the Business of Government, 2007), 6, https://www.researchgate.net/publication/272747065_The_Seven_Steps_of_Effective_Workforce_Planning.
8. Jennifer A. Alexander, John A. Ramsay, and Sue M. Thomson, "Designing the Health Workforce for the 21st Century," *Medical Journal of Australia* 180, no. 1 (2004): 7, https://doi.org/10.5694/j.1326-5377.2004.tb05764.x.
9. Alexander, Ramsay, and Thomson, "Designing the Health Workforce for the 21st Century."

10. David Tyack and William Tobin, "The 'Grammar' of Schooling: Why Has It Been so Hard to Change?," *American Educational Research Journal* 31, no. 3 (1994): 453–79, https://doi.org/10.3102/00028312031003453.
11. Tyack and Tobin, "The 'Grammar' of Schooling."
12. Tyack and Tobin, "The 'Grammar' of Schooling," 454.
13. Dan Lortie, *Schoolteacher: A Sociological Study* (Chicago: University of Chicago Press, 1975); Susan Moore Johnson, "Will VAMS Reinforce the Walls of the Egg-Crate School?," *Educational Researcher* 44, no. 2 (2015): 117–26, https://doi.org/10.3102/0013189X15573351; Susan Moore Johnson, *Where Teachers Thrive: Organizing Schools for Success* (Cambridge, MA: Harvard Education Press, 2019).
14. Tyack and Tobin, "The 'Grammar' of Schooling," 455.
15. Scott Emerick, Eric Hirsch, and Barnett Berry, *Teacher Working Conditions as Catalysts for Student Learning: Conditions for Learning*, Info Brief no. 43 (Alexandria, VA: Association for Supervision and Curriculum Development, October 2005), para. 3, ERIC Number: ED532701.
16. Jal Mehta and Sarah Fine, *In Search of Deeper Learning: The Quest to Remake the American High School* (Cambridge, MA: Harvard University Press, 2019), https://doi.org/10.4159/9780674239951; Jal Mehta and Amanda Datnow, "Changing the Grammar of Schooling: An Appraisal and a Research Agenda," *American Journal of Education* 126, no. 4 (2020): 1–5.
17. Brent W. Maddin and Randy L. Mahlerwein, "Empowering Educators Through Team-Based Staffing Models," *Phi Delta Kappan* 104, no. 1 (2022): 1–6, https://doi.org/10.1177/00317217221123647; Tim Walker, "Where Do Teachers Get the Most Respect?," *NEA Today*, November 28, 2018, https://www.nea.org/nea-today/all-news-articles/where-do-teachers-get-most-respect.
18. Labaree, "The Dynamic Tension at the Core of the Grammar of Schooling."
19. Linda Darling-Hammond et al., *Preparing Teachers for Deeper Learning: Research Brief* (Palo Alto, CA: Learning Policy Institute, June 2019), 1, https://learningpolicyinstitute.org/product/preparing-teachers-deeper-learning.
20. Django Paris and H. Samy Alim, eds., *Culturally Sustaining Pedagogies: Teaching and Learning for Justice in a Changing World* (New York: Teachers College Press, 2017).
21. Michael Fullan and Maria Langworthy, *A Rich Seam: How New Pedagogies Find Deep Learning* (London: Pearson, January 2014), 7, https://michaelfullan.ca/wp-content/uploads/2014/01/3897.Rich_Seam_web.pdf.
22. William and Flora Hewlett Foundation, "Deeper Learning Defined," April 23, 2013, https://www.hewlett.org/deeper-learning-defined/.
23. Darling-Hammond et al., *Preparing Teachers for Deeper Learning*, 3.
24. US Department of Education, Office of Educational Technology, *Transforming American Education: Learning Powered by Technology* (Washington, DC: US Department of Education, November 2010), https://www.ed.gov/technology/netp-2010.
25. Ling Zhang, James D. Basham, and Sohyun Yang, "Understanding the Implementation of Personalized Learning: A Research Synthesis," *Educational Research Review* 31 (November 2020): 100339, https://doi.org/10.1016/j.edurev.2020.100339.
26. Michael DeArmond and Tricia Maas, *Leading Personalized Learning* (Seattle: Center on Reinventing Public Education, September 2018), https://www.crpe.org/publications/leading-personalized-learning; James W. Keefe, "What Is Personalization?," *Phi Delta Kappan* 89, no. 3 (November 2007): 217–23, https://doi.org/10.1177/003172170708900311.

27. John F. Pane, Elizabeth D. Steiner, Matthew D. Baird, and Laura S. Hamilton, *Continued Progress: Promising Evidence on Personalized Learning* (Santa Monica, CA: RAND, November 2015), https://www.rand.org/pubs/research_reports/RR1365.html.
28. Pamela Cantor, Richard M. Lerner, Karen J. Pittman, Paul A. Chase, and Nora Gomperts, *Whole-Child Development, Learning, and Thriving: A Dynamic Systems Approach* (Cambridge: Cambridge University Press, 2021).
29. Deborah Loewenberg Ball and Francesca M. Forzani, "The Work of Teaching and the Challenge for Teacher Education," *Journal of Teacher Education* 60, no. 5 (November 2009): 497–511, https://doi.org/10.1177/0022487109348479.
30. Ball and Forzani, "The Work of Teaching and the Challenge for Teacher Education"; David F. Labaree, *The Trouble with Ed Schools* (New Haven, CT: Yale University Press, 2004); Lortie, *Schoolteacher*.
31. Gordon Mosser and James W. Begun, *Understanding Teamwork in Health Care* (New York: McGraw-Hill, 2014).
32. Johns Hopkins University Institute for Education Policy, "Results from the Year One Survey of Next Education Workforce Teachers," July 2022, https://workforce.education.asu.edu/resource/results-from-the-year-one-survey-of-next-education-workforce-teachers; Johns Hopkins University Institute for Education Policy, "Results from the Year Two Survey of Next Education Workforce Model Teachers," September 2023, https://workforce.education.asu.edu/resource/results-from-the-year-two-survey-of-next-education-workforce-teachers.
33. Specifically, researchers found that teachers in Next Education Workforce models take "one less day of leave and request substitute teachers for two fewer days per school year," 21. Alanna Bjorklund-Young, Angela R. Watson, and Al Passarella, *Next Education Workforce Model: An Examination of Teacher Engagement* (Baltimore, MD: Johns Hopkins University Institute for Education Policy, 2023), https://workforce.education.asu.edu/resource/an-examination-of-teacher-engagement-in-next-education-workforce-models.
34. Mary Laski, *Early Evidence of Improved Educator Outcomes in Next Education Workforce Models* (Seattle: Center on Reinventing Public Education, May 2024), https://crpe.org/early-evidence-of-improved-educator-outcomes-in-next-education-workforcetm-models/.
35. Richard Ingersoll, R. Lennon Audrain, and Mary Laski, *Team-Based Staffing, Teacher Autonomy, and Teacher Turnover* (Seattle: Center on Reinventing Public Education, forthcoming 2025).
36. Richard Ingersoll and R. Lennon Audrain, "What the Data Tell Us About Next Education Workforce Teachers in TSL Schools and Beyond," presentation at the Strategic School Staffing Summit, Arizona State University (ASU), February 7–8, 2024.
37. R. Lennon Audrain and Brent W. Maddin, *Third Grade Reading Growth in Next Education Workforce Models*, unpublished manuscript, Mary Lou Fulton College for Teaching and Learning Innovation, Arizona State University (ASU), 2023.
38. R. Lennon Audrain and Brent W. Maddin, *Algebra 1 Pass Rates in Next Education Workforce Models*, unpublished manuscript, Mary Lou Fulton College for Teaching and Learning Innovation, Arizona State University (ASU), 2022.
39. Audrain and Maddin, *Algebra 1 Pass Rates in Next Education Workforce Models*.
40. This set of funders included the Bill and Melinda Gates Foundation, the Carnegie Corporation of New York, the Joyce Foundation, the Overdeck Family Foundation, and Schusterman Family Philanthropies. Education First, "Strategic School Staffing Landscape Scan: Transforming School Staffing to Improve School Learning and Reimagine the Role of

Teachers," August 2023, https://www.education-first.com/wp-content/uploads/2023/12/EducationFirst_StrategicSchoolStaffingLandscapeScan.pdf.

41. Education First is a national strategy and policy organization dedicated to helping clients navigate through complexity to create more people-focused, equitable, and inclusive initiatives, strategies, and organizations, https://www.education-first.com; Education First, "Strategic School Staffing Landscape Scan."
42. Education First, "Strategic School Staffing Landscape Scan," 22.
43. Education First, "Strategic School Staffing Landscape Scan."
44. Education First, "Strategic School Staffing Landscape Scan," 50.
45. "Opportunity Culture Dashboard," Opportunity Culture, https://www.opportunityculture.org/dashboard/.
46. Examples of collaborative efforts between Public Impact and ASU's Next Education Workforce initiative include several coauthored grant proposals and helping to cofound the Coalition to Reimagine the Teaching Role, https://teachingrolereimagined.org.
47. For a more detailed history of team teaching in the mid-twentieth century, see R. Lennon Audrain's dissertation, "Looking Backward, Inward, and Forward: The Genealogy of, and Conceptual and Empirical Evidence for, the Next Education Workforce," PhD diss., Division for Advancing Education Policy, Practice and Leadership, Mary Lou Fulton College for Teaching and Learning Innovation, Arizona State University, 2023, https://keep.lib.asu.edu/items/187337.
48. Every Student Succeeds Act of 2015, Pub. L. No. 114-95, § 7801(42), 129 Stat. 1802 (2015).
49. Richard E. Elmore, "Improving the Instructional Core," in *Instructional Rounds in Education: A Network Approach to Improving Teaching and Learning*, ed. Elizabeth A. City, Richard E. Elmore, Sarah E. Fiarman, and Lee Teitel (Cambridge, MA: Harvard Education Press, 2009).
50. Barbara Bree Fischer, "A Clarification and Analysis of the Concept of Team Teaching in the Elementary School," EdD diss., University of Massachusetts Amherst, 1972, https://core.ac.uk/download/pdf/112623393.pdf.
51. Fischer, "A Clarification and Analysis of the Concept of Team Teaching," 5.

Chapter 1

1. Tim Walker, "Beyond Burnout: What Must Be Done to Tackle the Educator Shortage," NEA Today, April 14, 2022, https://www.nea.org/nea-today/all-news-articles/beyond-burnout-what-must-be-done-tackle-educator-shortage.
2. Gordon Mosser and James W. Begun, *Understanding Teamwork in Health Care* (New York: McGraw-Hill, 2014).
3. Steve W. J. Kozlowski and Daniel R. Ilgen, "Enhancing the Effectiveness of Work Groups and Teams," *Psychological Science in the Public Interest* 7, no. 3 (December 2006): 79, https://doi.org/10.1111/j.1529-1006.2006.00030.x.
4. Deborah Loewenberg Ball and Francesca M. Forzani, "The Work of Teaching and the Challenge for Teacher Education," *Journal of Teacher Education* 60, no. 5 (November 2009): 497–511, https://doi.org/10.1177/0022487109348479; David F. Labaree, *The Trouble with Ed Schools* (New Haven, CT: Yale University Press, 2004); Dan Lortie, *Schoolteacher: A Sociological Study* (Chicago: University of Chicago Press, 1975).
5. Daniel Weisberg et al., *The Widget Effect: Our National Failure to Acknowledge and Act on Differences in Teacher Effectiveness* (New York: New Teacher Project, 2009), https://www.widgeteffect.org.

6. World Health Organization, *Task Shifting: Rational Redistribution of Tasks Among Health Workforce Teams: Global Recommendations and Guidelines* (Geneva, Switzerland: World Health Organization, 2008), https://www.who.int/healthsystems/task_shifting/en/.
7. World Health Organization, *Task Shifting*, 2.
8. Jonathan A. Supovitz and Jolley Bruce Christman, *Developing Communities of Instructional Practice: Lessons from Cincinnati and Philadelphia*, CPRE Policy Briefs RB-39 (Philadelphia: Consortium for Policy Research in Education, November 2003), https://eric.ed.gov/?id=ED498331.
9. Matthew Ronfeldt, Susanna Owens Farmer, Kiel McQueen, and Jason A. Grissom, "Teacher Collaboration in Instructional Teams and Student Achievement," *American Educational Research Journal* 52, no. 3 (June 2015): 475–514, https://www.jstor.org/stable/24546739.
10. Ronfeldt et al., "Teacher Collaboration in Instructional Teams and Student Achievement."
11. Johns Hopkins University Institute for Education Policy, "Results from the Year One Survey of Next Education Workforce Teachers," July 2022, https://workforce.education.asu.edu/resource/results-from-the-year-one-survey-of-next-education-workforce-teachers; Johns Hopkins University Institute for Education Policy, "Results from the Year Two Survey of Next Education Workforce Model Teachers," September 2023, https://workforce.education.asu.edu/resource/results-from-the-year-two-survey-of-next-education-workforce-teachers.
12. City Year is a national service program that brings more than three thousand young adults from diverse backgrounds to support students of color and students from low-income backgrounds in dozens of cities across the United States. See more at https://www.cityyear.org/about/.
13. Education Professions is a career and technical education grow-your-own program for high school students. Grow-your-own programs seek to recruit and support future teachers from their local community. Skyline High School's Education Professions program joins Stevenson Elementary School's team-based staffing models to support educators in new roles. See more at R. Lennon Audrain, "A Cadre of Community Educators," Mary Lou Fulton College for Teaching and Learning Innovation, Tempe, AZ, November 17, 2022, https://education.asu.edu/about/news/cadre-community-educators.
14. Kozlowski and Ilgen, "Enhancing the Effectiveness of Work Groups and Teams."
15. See these texts for more information: Barnett Berry, *Teaching 2030: What We Must Do for Our Students and Our Public Schools—Now and in the Future* (New York: Teachers College Press, 2010); Frederick M. Hess, *The Great School Rethink* (Cambridge, MA: Harvard Education Press, 2023).
16. Center for Whole-Child Education, "Building Blocks for Learning," Arizona State University, Tempe, accessed August 8, 2024, https://turnaroundusa.org/what-we-do/tools/building-blocks/.
17. Julia Freeland Fisher, *Who You Know: Unlocking Innovations That Expand Students' Networks* (San Francisco: Jossey-Bass, 2018).
18. Ricardo D. Stanton-Salazar, "A Social Capital Framework for the Study of Institutional Agents and Their Role in the Empowerment of Low-Status Students and Youth," *Youth & Society* 43, no. 3 (2011): 1066–1109.
19. Dylan Wiliam and Siobhán Leahy, *Embedding Formative Assessment: Practical Techniques for K–12 Classrooms* (Bloomington, IN: Solution Tree, 2024).
20. "Why Having a Best Friend at Work Is Important," *Gallup* (blog), December 5, 2022, https://www.gallup.com/cliftonstrengths/en/406298/why-having-best-friend-work-important.aspx.

21. National Center for Education Statistics (NCES), "Most Public Schools Face Challenges in Hiring Teachers and Other Personnel Entering the 2023–24 Academic Year," press release, October 17, 2023, https://nces.ed.gov/whatsnew/press_releases/10_17_2023.asp.

Chapter 2

1. Douglas McCarthy, Kimberly Mueller, and Jennifer Wrenn, *Mayo Clinic: Multidisciplinary Teamwork, Physician-Led Governance, and Patient-Centered Culture Drive World-Class Health Care* (New York: Commonwealth Fund, August 2009), https://www.commonwealthfund.org/publications/case-study/2009/aug/mayo-clinic.
2. Ray R. Buss, "Using Action Research as a Signature Pedagogy to Develop EdD Students' Inquiry as Practice Abilities," *Impacting Education: Journal on Transforming Professional Practice* 3, no. 1 (2018), https://doi.org/10.5195/ie.2018.46.
3. Mesa Public Schools, "Portrait of a Graduate," accessed August 8, 2024, https://www.mpsaz.org/page/portrait.
4. Gregory A. Mendez, "Implementation and Evaluation of a Teams-Based Approach at an Alternative High School," EdD diss., Arizona State University, 2023, 5, https://keep.lib.asu.edu/taxonomy/term/155630.
5. Mendez, "Implementation and Evaluation of a Teams-Based Approach at an Alternative High School."
6. Victoria Boyd, *School Context: Bridge or Barrier for Change?* (Austin, TX: Southwest Educational Development Laboratory, 1992), https://eric.ed.gov/?id=ED370216.

Chapter 3

1. Michaeleen Doucleff, "The Doctor Who Championed Hand-Washing and Saved Women's Lives," NPR, January 12, 2015, https://www.npr.org/sections/health-shots/2015/01/12/375663920/the-doctor-who-championed-hand-washing-and-saved-women-s-lives; Uvi Tyagi and Kailash Chander Barwal, "Ignac Semmelweis—Father of Hand Hygiene," *Indian Journal of Surgery* 82, no. 3 (June 2020): 276–77, https://doi.org/10.1007/s12262-020-02386-6.
2. John P. Kotter, *8 Steps to Accelerate Change in Your Organization* (Kotter Inc., 2018), https://www.kotterinc.com/wp-content/uploads/2019/04/8-Steps-eBook-Kotter-2018.pdf.
3. Everett M. Rogers, *Diffusion of Innovations*, 5th ed. (New York: Free Press, 2003).
4. Kotter, *8 Steps to Accelerate Change in Your Organization*, 11.
5. Kotter, *8 Steps to Accelerate Change in Your Organization*, 10.
6. Kotter, *8 Steps to Accelerate Change in Your Organization*, 13.
7. Kotter, *8 Steps to Accelerate Change in Your Organization*, 18.
8. Ronald A. Heifetz, *Leadership Without Easy Answers* (Cambridge, MA: Harvard University Press, 1994).
9. Ronald A. Heifetz and Marty Linsky, "A Survival Guide for Leaders," *Harvard Business Review*, June 2002, https://hbr.org/2002/06/a-survival-guide-for-leaders.
10. Heifetz and Linsky, "A Survival Guide for Leaders."
11. Heifetz and Linsky, "A Survival Guide for Leaders."
12. Rogers, *Diffusion of Innovations*.
13. Rogers, *Diffusion of Innovations*.
14. Rogers, *Diffusion of Innovations*.
15. We don't find the term "laggards" especially helpful, so we have changed it to "last adopters."

Chapter 4

1. Walter Isaacson, *Steve Jobs* (New York: Simon & Schuster, 2011).

Chapter 5

1. Joe D. Nichols, "Scheduling Reform: A Longitudinal Exploration of High School Block Scheduling Structures," *International Journal of Educational Reform* 9, no. 2 (April 2000): 105–17, https://doi.org/10.1177/105678790000900205.
2. *Design Principles for Schools: Putting the Science of Learning and Development into Action: Rich Learning Experiences and Knowledge Development* (Learning Policy Institute and Turnaround for Children, September 2021), 60, https://learningpolicyinstitute.org/sites/default/files/product-files/SoLD_Design_Principles_Principle_3_Rich_Learning.pdf.
3. Beth C. Rubin and Pedro A. Noguera, "Tracking Detracking: Sorting Through the Dilemmas and Possibilities of Detracking in Practice," *Equity & Excellence in Education* 37, no. 1 (2004): 92–101, https://doi.org/10.1080/10665680490422142.
4. "Innovating Arizona's Education Model to Meet the Needs of Individual Students," Center for the Future of Arizona (blog), July 2022, https://www.arizonafuture.org/news-events/news/2022/7/innovating-arizona-s-education-model-to-meet-the-needs-of-individual-students/.

Chapter 6

1. Felichism W. Kabo et al., "Proximity Effects on the Dynamics and Outcomes of Scientific Collaborations," *Research Policy* 43, no. 9 (November 2014): 1469–85, https://doi.org/10.1016/j.respol.2014.04.007.
2. Robert Dillon and Rebecca Hare, *The Space: A Guide for Leaders* (EdTech Press, 2016).
3. "Ehrman Crest Elementary/Middle School," *Time*, November 10, 2022, https://time.com/collection/best-inventions-2022/6228824/ehrman-crest-elementary-middle-school/.

Chapter 7

1. Apurva Pamidimukkala et al., "Evaluation of Barriers to Electric Vehicle Adoption: A Study of Technological, Environmental, Financial, and Infrastructure Factors," *Transportation Research Interdisciplinary Perspectives* 22 (November 2023): 100962, https://doi.org/10.1016/j.trip.2023.100962.
2. *Teachers Know Best: Teachers' Views on Professional Development* (Seattle: Bill & Melinda Gates Foundation, December 2014), https://s3.amazonaws.com/edtech-production/reports/Gates-PDMarketResearch-Dec5.pdf.
3. Matthew A. Kraft, David Blazar, and Dylan Hogan, "The Effect of Teacher Coaching on Instruction and Achievement: A Meta-Analysis of the Causal Evidence," *Review of Educational Research* 88, no. 4 (December 2018): 547–88, https://doi.org/10.3102/0034654318759268.

Chapter 8

1. The What Works Clearinghouse defines career academies as "school-within-school programs operating in high schools . . . students in career academies take both career-related and academic courses and acquire work experience through partnerships with local employers," https://ies.ed.gov/ncee/WWC/InterventionReport/70.

2. Daniel T. Holt, Achilles A. Armenakis, Hubert S. Feild, and Stanley G. Harris, "Readiness for Organizational Change: The Systematic Development of a Scale," *Journal of Applied Behavioral Science* 43, no. 2 (June 2007): 232–55, https://doi.org/10.1177/0021886306295295.
3. Holt et al., "Readiness for Organizational Change," 232.
4. Holt et al., "Readiness for Organizational Change," 238.
5. Holt et al., "Readiness for Organizational Change," 238.
6. Holt et al., "Readiness for Organizational Change," 239.

Acknowledgments

In 2016, Dr. Carole Basile became dean of the Mary Lou Fulton College for Teaching and Learning Innovation. In this role, she has lived up to Arizona State University (ASU)'s reputation as "#1 in Innovation." It was she who first asked the question about whether our education workforce could be redesigned to deliver reliably better outcomes for both educators and students. Carole, thank you for setting a bold vision, continually asking the hard questions, and helping to build the Next Education Workforce.

As this book goes to print, the Next Education Workforce initiative team has supported more than fifty school systems on their journey to design team-based school staffing models. This would not have been possible without the leadership and collaboration of our first two school-system partners, Kyrene School District and Mesa Public Schools, and the inspiring leadership of their respective superintendents, Drs. Jan Vesely and Andi Fourlis. You both set the standard for what partnership looks like.

To all the educators from whom we've learned over the years, thank you. We would specifically like to recognize all of those who provided feedback on early versions of this manuscript and shared their insights in the pages that follow. Your concrete stories bring life and authenticity to this volume. Specifically, we'd like to recognize and thank all of those who are quoted in the book for their contributions.

Ultimately, this is a book about the power of educator teams, and we are so grateful to our teammates, past and present, at the Next Education Workforce initiative, the Mary Lou Fulton College for Teaching and Learning Innovation, and ASU. All told, there are more than one hundred teammates who have contributed either directly or indirectly to this manuscript. We would like to specifically recognize a few who helped us out on a few particularly tricky sections: Colleen Broderick, Kevin Corner, Andrea LaRocca, and Brad Thompson. Thank you.

Finally, each of us would like to recognize our families, friends, and pets who provided support and love in immeasurable ways. To Christine, Scott, Alice, Carol, Rob, Diane, Pat, Larry, Amanda, David, Charlie, Henry, Evie, Odie, Matt, Brad, Wattanee, Heather, MaryJo, Sofia, Emily, Patch, Gradie, Poppy Mae, Carol, Cindy, Kenny, Steve, and Marucela, thank you.

Writing this book with the input and support from so many incredible people made this project a true pleasure. It literally would not have been possible without them. That said, any errors or shortcomings are the responsibility of the authors alone.

To our readers, we hope that you find inspiration and concrete, actionable resources in the pages that follow. If what you read here helps you launch or refine a team-based approach to school staffing, let us know! We can't wait to learn with and from you.

About the Authors

Brent W. Maddin

As executive director of the Next Education Workforce, Brent W. Maddin collaborates with colleagues across Arizona State University (ASU), P12 educators, and the community to redesign models of schooling based on teams of educators with distributed expertise who are better able to deliver on the promise of deeper and personalized learning for *all* students. In addition, these team-based models help address many of the reasons why educators leave teaching by creating more equitable and sustainable ways to enter and advance in the profession.

Prior to coming to ASU, Maddin was a cofounder of and provost at the Relay Graduate School of Education, where he set the curricular vision for the institution and managed teams focused on curriculum design, institutional research, and programmatic innovation. While at Relay, Maddin also founded TeacherSquared, a national center dedicated to increasing collaboration among teacher preparation institutions. Prior to helping launch TeacherSquared and Relay, Maddin earned a doctorate from the Harvard Graduate School of Education, served as a founding staff member at IDEA College Prep, and was a National Board-Certified Teacher in secondary science.

He also previously coauthored the following book: Carole G. Basile, Brent W. Maddin, and R. Lennon Audrain, *The Next Education Workforce: How Team-Based Staffing Models Can Support Equity and Improve Learning Outcomes* (Lanham, MD: Rowman & Littlefield, 2022).

R. Lennon Audrain

Richard "Lennon" Audrain, an enrolled member of the Cherokee Nation and Shawnee Tribe, is a research assistant professor at ASU's Mary Lou Fulton College for Teaching and Learning Innovation. He led the strategy on the Next Education Workforce initiative's Teacher and School Leader grant, an $8.2 million US Department of Education grant awarded to ASU in partnership with Mesa Public Schools to redesign the district's human capital management systems in support of team-based staffing models. Audrain taught Latin, Spanish, English, and a career and technical education grow-your-own program in both Arizona and Massachusetts.

Audrain's research interests explore two features of the education workforce: human capital management systems and systems of teacher education. As the product of a high school grow-your-own program and the former national president of Educators Rising, Audrain's particular interest explores teacher recruitment, preparation, in-service professional learning, career advancement, and working conditions—and how these shift when schools and school systems adopt team-based staffing models.

Audrain earned his PhD in educational policy and evaluation from ASU in May 2023. He was the youngest graduate from both his master's classes at ASU and Harvard University. He earned his first master's degree in curriculum and instruction from ASU at age nineteen, and his second master's degree in technology, innovation, and education from the Harvard Graduate School of Education at age twenty-one.

He also previously coauthored the following book: Carole G. Basile, Brent W. Maddin, and R. Lennon Audrain, *The Next Education Workforce: How Team-Based Staffing Models Can Support Equity and Improve Learning Outcomes* (Lanham, MD: Rowman & Littlefield, 2022).

Lisa Maresso Wyatt

As senior director of implementation and design, Lisa Maresso Wyatt leads the team's support for schools and systems exploring and implementing Next Education Workforce team-based models. She sets the strategic direction for, and oversees the operationalization of, the scaled support that the Next Education Workforce team offers, including professional learning, direct technical assistance, and resource development for PK–12 schools and systems. Wyatt works with the executive director and senior director of strategy and operation to strategically design systems and structures that meet a large, and expanding, national demand for Next Education Workforce models. She has over twenty-five years of experience in PK–12 and higher education. Prior to joining ASU, Wyatt was a teacher and leader in elementary, high school, and community college settings for twenty years. An Arizona native and former Peace Corps volunteer, Wyatt holds a bachelor of arts degree in English from the University of

San Diego and a master's of education degree from the University of California, Los Angeles (UCLA).

Kaycee Salmacia

As senior director of Partnerships, Strategy & Operations, Kaycee Salmacia sets vision and direction for the team's national strategy and business model and leads the day-to-day operations of the Next Education Workforce team. Salmacia oversees the team's inquiry-to-impact pipeline ensuring meaningful opportunities for school systems across the country to learn about Next Education Workforce models, partner with ASU to implement models in their context, and measure progress and impact of their shared work.

Prior to joining the Next Education Workforce, Salmacia served as vice provost and chief academic compliance officer at the Relay Graduate School of Education overseeing authorization and accreditation of Relay's regional campuses and academic programs. As a faculty member, Salmacia's teaching and research focused on helping novice educators become outcome-driven, data-literate teachers. Prior to Salmacia's work in higher education, she spent a decade in K–12 education as a tutor, middle school teacher, and teacher coach. Salmacia holds a master of arts degree in teaching from Pace University and a doctorate in higher education management from the University of Pennsylvania.

Index